FORMULA ONE 2021

Published in 2021 by Welbeck

An Imprint of Welbeck Non-Fiction Limited, part of Welbeck Publishing Group.
20 Mortimer Street London W1T 3JW

The publisher has taken reasonable steps to check the accuracy of the facts contained herein at the time of going to press, but can take no responsibility for any errors.

A CIP catalogue record for this book is available from the British Library

ISBN 978-1-78739-572-5

Project Editor: Ross Hamilton
Design: Luke Griffin
Picture Research: Paul Langan
Production: Rachel Burgess

Printed in Spain

10 9 8 7 6 5 4

MIX
Paper from responsible sources
FSC® C009279

Above: History-maker Lewis Hamilton celebrates claiming his record-equalling seventh World Championship alongside Sebastian Vettel, Toto Wolff and Sergio Perez at the Turkish GP.

FORMULA ONE 2021

TEAMS | DRIVERS | TRACKS | RECORDS

BRUCE JONES

WELBECK

» CONTENTS

Right: Max Verstappen celebrates his first win of 2020 at Silverstone's 70th Anniversary GP.

A notable feature of grids in 2020 was how social distancing rules restricted access only to teams.

» ANALYSIS OF THE 2021 SEASON

It was supposed to have been all change for 2021, with the Formula One World Championship adopting a long-planned and much-needed budget cap of $175m and a whole raft of new technical changes that might shake up the order. Instead, because of the strictures of Covid-19, the changes have been held back until next year, and so Mercedes has every reason to be delighted, as it can race on with its dominant package.

Mercedes is keeping its winning formula, for one more season at least, with Lewis Hamilton electing to continue so that he can take a tilt at landing a record eighth F1 title after a period last year when he talked of maybe doing something else. Few felt that he would make that move away when he stood on the brink of becoming the driver with the most-ever F1 titles. Valtteri Bottas has a one-year contract extension but can harbour few hopes that he will ever be anything other than the number two driver, and so have to tolerate those occasionally sacrificial race strategies he gets put onto when conditions are changeable.

A cloud fell over Red Bull Racing in 2020 when Honda announced that it would be quitting F1 at the end of this year, leaving the team in need of a new engine deal from an increasingly shallow pool of candidates. Max Verstappen is sure to be as mighty as ever, leaving Sergio Perez to attempt to get close to his pace, something that none have managed yet.

Aston Martin is not a new name in the World Championship as it was part of the show in 1959 and 1960. However, it's back as the new name of the team that started life in 1991 as Jordan and shone last year as Racing Point. Lance Stroll returns for more, anxious to keep the momentum going and build on his surprise pole in the Turkish GP. Many felt it wrong that Sergio Perez was dropped, but Aston Martin welcomes Sebastian Vettel in his place. The four-time world champion arrives chastened from a

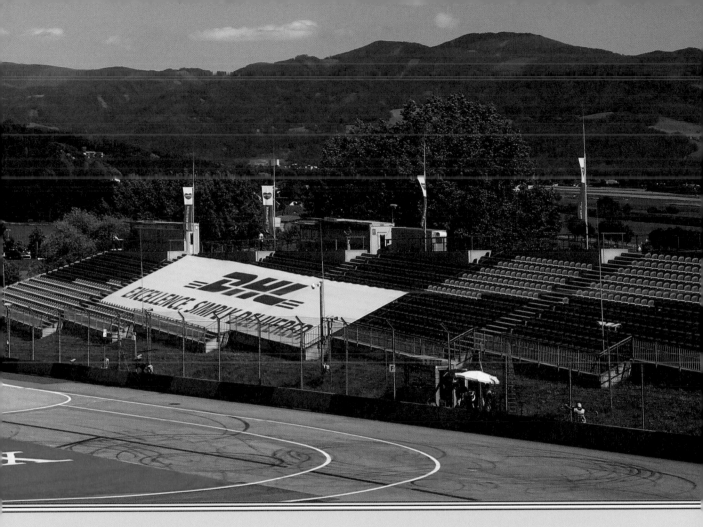

poor final year with Ferrari and could be one of the main players in 2021 if he bounces back.

McLaren has also undergone change as it welcomes Daniel Ricciardo alongside Lando Norris, and the smiling Australian has picked a good time to join the team from Woking as its form and confidence are both burgeoning.

Like Racing Point, the Renault team of last year has a new name: Alpine. This is in deference to the French manufacturer's long-time sports car marque. With Ricciardo's departure, Esteban Ocon might have expected that he would lead the attack, but the return to F1 of Fernando Alonso ought to challenge that concept. For the oft-thwarted Spaniard, he will relish having a car that ought to give him more of a chance than the McLaren that held him back on his last F1 foray in 2018.

Ferrari is in the doldrums, with its weak showing in 2020 not likely to be improved upon enormously this year as the planned F1 technical rule changes have been shelved until 2022. Charles Leclerc will continue to take his Ferrari as high up the order as it deserves to go, but there will be a new dynamic provided by the arrival of Carlos Sainz Jr from McLaren.

AlphaTauri is unlikely to have another day of days after Pierre Gasly's extraordinary win at Monza last year, but Gasly is happy to stay here rather than return to Red Bull Racing as number two to Verstappen. Yuki Tsunoda has been signed to drive the second car.

Alfa Romeo is a shadow of what the Italian manufacturer must have hoped it would be when it took over the naming rights for the Swiss team known formerly as Sauber. Kimi Raikkonen and Antonio Giovinazzi have been retained, while Haas F1 has taken the opposite approach and has opted to discard Romain Grosjean and Kevin Magnussen and replace them with a pair of F1 rookies, Mick Schumacher and Nikita Mazepin, with the former coming with the blessing of engine supplier Ferrari.

It took a buy-out to keep Williams on the grid for 2021, with the family stepping down and new money and ideas arriving in their place. George Russell and Nicholas Latifi stay on and have the same goal: to score points.

With everything in the world, let alone just sport, going through considerable turmoil and uncertainty, one great piece of news last September was the appointment of Stefano Domenicali as Formula One's new boss. This former Ferrari team principal was brought back into the fold after five years away, during which he became chief executive of Lamborghini, to take the helm from Chase Carey.

As good a job as the American has done since taking the helm in 2017, people expect the personable Domenicali to have his finger on the pulse for the years ahead as F1 fights to keep itself affordable, exciting and relevant to the mores of the age.

MERCEDES-AMG PETRONAS

It's said that success breeds success in sport and that can often be true, but this team stays at the top due to a combination of excellent technical staff, top drivers, a healthy budget and a determination never to stand still.

Lewis Hamilton enjoyed a record-breaking season in 2020 and has every expectation of doing the same for Mercedes to go for an eighth title.

So comprehensive and enduring has been the Mercedes F1 team's domination of the World Championship since 2014 that it's hard sometimes to recall that this is a team that had to work its way through three previous guises to reach its current pace-setting position.

Life for today's silver-liveried serial champions began in F1 in a very different manner. This was back in 1999 when the defunct Tyrrell team's championship entry was bought by a consortium led by Craig Pollock and 1997 World Champion Jacques Villeneuve. Between them, they formed a new team called British American Racing, BAR, in deference to its tobacco sponsor. Perhaps they were visionaries, for they used a tagline that is certainly applicable now, but wasn't then. It is "a tradition of excellence".

Despite its healthy budget and tailor-made headquarters at Brackley near Silverstone, Villeneuve and team-mate Ricardo Zonta struggled through that first campaign, seldom finishing. Yet, bit by

bit, BAR got closer to the pace and had a brilliant season in 2004 when Jenson Button guided the team to second overall thanks to taking four second-place finishes in a year dominated by Michael Schumacher and Ferrari.

Tumbling to sixth overall in 2005 after failing to score a single point until the

KEY PERSONNEL & 2020 ROUND-UP

MIKE ELLIOTT

The team's technology director trained as an aeronautical engineer then, encouraged by a fellow student to take those skills to F1, he joined McLaren in 2000, moved to Renault in 2008 and then to Mercedes in 2012 as head of aerodynamics. With huge success since the start of F1's hybrid era in 2014, his years with the silver arrows have been golden. Promotion to technology director in 2017 has given Elliott increasing responsibility.

MERCEDES MAKES IT SEVEN TITLES IN A ROW

Valtteri Bottas won the opening race, but last year was always going to be about Lewis Hamilton extending his amazing winning streak and he duly delivered. The Mercedes F1 W11 was simply too good for the nine rival teams and win followed win. There were times when Lewis clearly had to stretch himself, like when tyre problems emerged at Silverstone, but often he made it look effortless. With major technical rule changes delayed until 2022, the team is well set for another year of glory this year.

2020 DRIVERS & RESULTS

Driver	Nationality	Races	Wins	Pts	Pos
Lewis Hamilton	British	16	11	347	1st
Valtteri Bottas	Finnish	17	2	223	2nd
George Russell	British	1	0	3	18th

FOR THE RECORD

Country of origin:	England
Team base:	Brackley, England
Telephone:	(44) 01280 844000
Website:	www.mercedes-amg-f1.com

Active in Formula One:
As BAR 1999-2005, Honda Racing
2006-08, Brawn GP 2009, Mercedes
2010 on

Grands Prix contested:	403
Wins:	115
Pole positions:	126
Fastest laps:	84

THE TEAM

Head of Mercedes-Benz Motorsport:	Toto Wolff
Technical director:	James Allison
MD, Mercedes-AMG High Performance powertrains:	Hywel Thomas
Director of digital engineering:	Geoff Willis
Technology director:	Mike Elliott
Engineering director:	John Owen
Performance director:	Loic Serra
Sporting director:	Ron Meadows
Chief race engineer:	Andrew Shovlin
Chief track engineer:	Simon Cole
Test driver:	Stoffel Vandoorne
Chassis:	Mercedes F1 W12
Engine:	Mercedes V6
Tyres:	Pirelli

second half of the year wasn't part of the plan, and it proved a game-changer as BAR was no more in 2006, the team taken over by its engine supplier to become Honda Racing. With Button being joined by Rubens Barrichello, progress was expected, and a first win was achieved by Button in Hungary, charging from 14th to first in a wet race.

Unfortunately, fourth in 2006 was followed by eighth in 2007 and ninth in 2008, which was not the progression that Honda had sought. Combined with the global economic slump, Honda announced late in 2008 that it was pulling out. This left the team on the brink of extinction, but technical director Ross Brawn took control, had to make 200 staff redundant so that it could survive, and had a scrambled preparation for the 2009 season when it would race as Brawn GP.

What followed was extraordinary, as aerodynamicist Ben Wood produced a masterstroke in designing a double-decked diffuser that made the car the class of the field. Button guided his Mercedes-powered BGP 001 to six wins in the first seven rounds before the rivals caught up. Barrichello added two wins later in the year, but Brawn GP resisted Red Bull Racing's late charge to win the Constructors' Cup at its first attempt, with Button the drivers' champ too.

For 2010, though, Brawn GP was no more, with the cars painted silver for Mercedes as it became a works entity for the first time in 55 years. The team had closed its doors as a result of the 1955 Le Mans disaster that left as many as 100 dead after one of its cars was catapulted into the crowd. Seven-time world champion Michael Schumacher was brought back from retirement and was joined by Nico Rosberg, but the results were not glorious as the team ranked only fourth, with Rosberg outscoring Schumacher. Fourth again in 2011 and fifth in 2012, despite Rosberg claiming victory in China, the team dropped Schumacher and signed Lewis Hamilton from McLaren for 2013 and progress was finally made, edging out Ferrari to finish the year second.

Then came 2014 and Mercedes-AMG Petronas had finally arrived, as Hamilton began a run of seven championship titles – six for him and one in 2016 for Rosberg – to make Mercedes one of the greatest teams in F1 history. Racer turned business tycoon Toto Wolff leads the team and in James Allison he has one of the best technical directors in the business, with continuity of staff another of the keys to success.

"We never play politics inside the team, as empowering people is most important to us. Ours is a fun place, but also a pushy place. We save the politics to play outside."

Toto Wolff

Nico Rosberg leads Michael Schumacher on his way to victory in China in 2012, its first as Mercedes.

LEWIS HAMILTON

Lewis drove better than ever before last year as he raced to his seventh F1 title. This was bad news for his rivals and shows how he races himself as much as them as he strives for more wins and more records.

Lewis rose to even greater heights in 2020 and yet his hunger remains strong for more.

From the moment he turned from racing radio-control cars to race karts, Lewis has been a trailblazer, filling his career tally with wins and titles.

Lewis became cadet champion when 10, then used the opportunity of meeting McLaren boss Ron Dennis to elicit support for the rest of his kart career. Dennis's decision to do this in return for a long-term contract was a wise one.

At the end of 2001, he tried Formula Renault and won the British title in his second full season. Formula Three then came and went, before Lewis won the GP2 crown at his first attempt in 2006.

Lewis was ready for F1, then showed on his debut that F1 wasn't quite ready for him as he drove past established stars at the start in Australia. He appeared equal to the very best and took on his team-mate, double world champion Fernando Alonso. The first win came in Canada, and three more by year's end gave him a title shot, but he and Alonso ended up one point short of Ferrari's Kimi Raikkonen.

That was impressive, but Lewis wasted no time in landing his first F1 title in 2008, albeit doing so with a passing move on the last lap of the last race.

Wins kept on coming, but McLaren was outpaced by Brawn GP in 2009 and then by Red Bull Racing.

Seeking further titles, Lewis joined Mercedes in 2013 as it hit regular winning form. Then came the titles, in 2014 and 2015, but he was pipped by his karting team-mate Nico Rosberg in 2016, before adding four more through to 2020.

MATCHING SCHUMACHER'S TALLY

Records are there to be beaten, and Lewis was aware of that as he broke yet more in 2020. However, those are side benefits to Lewis, as each year's focus is winning the title. And this he did. It wasn't all plain sailing, as shown by his stumble in Austria when he was penalized for causing a collision and fell to fourth. In Russia he got a penalty after performing practice starts in an illegal part of the track (on wrong advice from his team) and in the Italian GP he entered the pits when they were closed, causing him to finish seventh. These glitches aside, he kept on coming out on top. Even in the British GP, where his front left tyre blew on the final lap, he was still able to limp on to victory. In the other races, though, Lewis always had enough in hand to keep stretching his points advantage over Mercedes team-mate Valtteri Bottas. With no team threatening Mercedes, he took his seventh F1 title to match Michael Schumacher's long-standing record, having passed the German's total of 91 GP wins.

TRACK NOTES

Nationality:	**BRITISH**
Born:	**7 JANUARY 1985,**
	STEVENAGE, ENGLAND
Website:	**www.lewishamilton.com**
Teams:	**McLAREN 2007-12,**
	MERCEDES 2013-21

CAREER RECORD

First Grand Prix: **2007 AUSTRALIAN GP**

Grand Prix starts: **266**

Grand Prix wins: **95**
2007 Canadian GP, United States GP, Hungarian GP, Japanese GP, 2008 Australian GP, Monaco GP, British GP, German GP, Chinese GP, 2009 Hungarian GP, Singapore GP, 2010 Turkish GP, Canadian GP, Belgian GP, 2011 Chinese GP, German GP, Abu Dhabi GP, 2012 Canadian GP, Hungarian GP, Italian GP, United States GP, 2013 Hungarian GP, 2014 Malaysian GP, Bahrain GP, Chinese GP, Spanish GP, British GP, Italian GP, Singapore GP, Japanese GP, Russian GP, United States GP, Abu Dhabi GP, 2015 Australian GP, Chinese GP, Bahrain GP, Canadian GP, British GP, Belgian GP, Italian GP, Japanese GP, Russian GP, United States GP, 2016 Monaco GP, Canadian GP, Austrian GP, British GP, Hungarian GP, German GP, United States GP, Mexican GP, Brazilian GP, Abu Dhabi GP, 2017 Chinese GP, Spanish GP, Canadian GP, British GP, Belgian GP, Italian GP, Singapore GP, Japanese GP, United States GP, 2018 Azerbaijan GP, Spanish GP, French GP, German GP, Hungarian GP, Italian GP, Singapore GP, Russian GP, Japanese GP, Brazilian GP, Abu Dhabi GP, 2019 Bahrain GP, Chinese GP, Spanish GP, Monaco GP, Canadian GP, French GP, British GP, Hungarian GP, Russian GP, Mexican GP, Abu Dhabi GP, 2020 Styrian GP, Hungarian GP, British GP, Spanish GP, Belgian GP, Tuscan GP, Eifel GP, Portuguese GP, Emilia Romagna GP, Turkish GP, Bahrain GP

Poles:	**98**
Fastest laps:	**53**
Points:	**3778**

Honours: **2008, 2014, 2015, 2017, 2018, 2019 & 2020 F1 WORLD CHAMPION, 2007 & 2016 F1 RUNNER-UP, 2006 GP2 CHAMPION, 2005 EUROPEAN F3 CHAMPION, 2003 BRITISH FORMULA RENAULT CHAMPION, 2000 WORLD KART CUP & EUROPEAN FORMULA A KART CHAMPION, 1999 ITALIAN INTERCON A CHAMPION, 1995 BRITISH CADET KART CHAMPION**

VALTTERI BOTTAS

It was like groundhog day for this flying Finn in 2020 as, just like in 2019, he won the opening round but then was pushed back into the shade at Mercedes by Lewis Hamilton. Even with a midseason slump, he ranked second.

Valtteri showed that, on his day, he can beat Lewis. He now wants more of those days.

What many fans don't realize is just how much of an investment families of racing prodigies put into their offspring. Not just in terms of finance but in time too, as they criss-cross their countries. The more they succeed, the more they have to travel as national competitions are superseded by international ones. If you come from Finland, the journeys are appreciably longer than for other European karting stars.

Yet, Valtteri persevered and was able to make the jump into single-seater racing at 17 in 2007. He started in Formula Renault and, in his second year, pipped Daniel Ricciardo to the European title.

F3 was next and Valtteri was quick enough to twice rank third in the European series, taking the annual Marlboro Masters race each year as a consolation prize.

In 2011, Valtteri would have liked to have advanced to GP2 but lacked the funds and so moved almost sideways to GP3. What he had to do was win the title and this he did and, with it, an F1 test drive with Williams. This proved to be a godsend, as Valtteri impressed the team so much that it put him onto its books as a test driver. So, in 2012, Valtteri took part in several of the Friday morning practice sessions at grands prix.

This earned Valtteri a race seat for 2013 and he struggled through a year when Renault engines weren't the ones to have. In 2014, Williams ran with Mercedes power and Valtteri responded in style by going up 13 places in the rankings to fourth overall.

Fifth in 2015 was followed by eighth in 2016 and then, at the 11th hour, a dream switch to Mercedes when Nico Rosberg quit suddenly after landing the title.

So, this meant playing second fiddle to Lewis Hamilton, a driver already with three F1 titles to his name, and little has changed since then, despite Valtteri taking the first of his nine wins to date in the first year racing a Silver Arrow.

TRACK NOTES

Nationality:	**FINNISH**
Born:	**28 AUGUST 1989, NASTOLA, FINLAND**
Website:	**www.valtteribottas.com**
Teams:	**WILLIAMS 2013-16, MERCEDES 2017-21**

CAREER RECORD

First Grand Prix:	**2013 AUSTRALIAN GP**
Grand Prix starts:	**156**
Grand Prix wins:	**9**
	2017 Russian GP, Austrian GP, Abu Dhabi GP, 2019 Australian GP, Azerbaijan GP, Japanese GP, US GP, 2020 Austrian GP, Russian GP
Poles:	**16**
Fastest laps:	**15**
Points:	**1512**
Honours:	**2019 & 2020 F1 RUNNER-UP, 2011 GP3 CHAMPION, 2009 & 2010 FORMULA 3 MASTERS WINNER, 2008 EUROPEAN & NORTHERN EUROPEAN FORMULA RENAULT CHAMPION**

ANOTHER YEAR, THE SAME OLD STORY

Pole position for the delayed opening round of the season in Austria was a fillip, and it felt better still when Valtteri led every lap as he raced to victory. Having had to play second fiddle to Lewis Hamilton for the previous three seasons, he might have smirked a little when his team-mate was penalized and pushed down to fourth place, enabling him to open out a points lead. However, then came the inevitable response as Lewis won the next three rounds on the trot. At the third of these, the British GP, Valtteri failed to score when he had a blow-out and had to limp back to the pits, falling to 12th by the time he got there. After this, there was the traditional run of second places, but also a trio of thirds and a fifth as Max Verstappen in particular got ever more competitive in his Red Bull. But a second win of 2020 in round 10, the Russian GP, restored a little of Valtteri's pride. He started setting poles again, but Lewis was always that bit better in the races.

Artistic reflections of the cars in an unusually sunlit pitlane at Silverstone.

>> RED BULL RACING

This year marks Red Bull Racing's final season with Honda, as the manufacturer is quitting F1 at the end of the campaign, so perhaps the biggest battle will be to secure an engine supplier, with Sergio Perez joining for 2021 to add points.

Max Verstappen was the chief Mercedes chaser in 2020 and, with a freeze on technical change, is more than likely to be doing that again in 2021.

Jackie Stewart is not just a three-time World Champion, but a champion in business too, fastidious in all he does, each day divided into bite-size chunks, and all filled with achievement. This year will mark 48 years since his final grand prix, but he is still involved with F1, representing blue-chip sponsors, still an insider.

Back in 1997, Jackie and elder son Paul moved up from F3000 into F1, upgrading its facilities in Milton Keynes accordingly and signing Rubens Barrichello and Jan Magnussen to lead its attack. Immaculately turned out, as one would expect, the white cars with the tartan detailing were competitive and surprised everyone when the Brazilian finished second at Monaco. Then, in a wet/dry race at the Nurburgring in 1999, Johnny Herbert led Barrichello in a Stewart one-three. This ought to have set the team up for greater things, but Jackie realized that more money was required to rise above that season's ranking of fourth.

So, the team was sold to Ford and rebadged Jaguar Racing to help promote its subsidiary. With the cars now metallic dark green, there were flashes of speed from Eddie Irvine and Mark Webber, with a best result of third place for the Ulsterman in the 2001 Monaco GP. However, there was a pressure that has never worked

KEY PERSONNEL & 2020 ROUND-UP

CHRISTIAN HORNER
Christian is known for tapping his foot nervously during races, hoping that his strategy will outflank Mercedes. He is also, in his own mind, out there doing the driving, as Christian was a racer, competing all the way up to Formula 3000. Then he turned to management with the family's Arden team, twice landing the F3000 crown. His big break came when Red Bull wanted its own team and he was brought in to transform it from Jaguar Racing.

SUCCEEDING FERRARI AS BEST OF THE REST
From the delayed outset of the season, it was clear that Mercedes was again the class of the field. The big question was which team would lead the perhaps futile chase. Ferrari was off the pace, so Red Bull Racing stepped up, with Max Verstappen leading the way. He might have won the British GP, but Lewis Hamilton limped home first. A week later, again at Silverstone, it was Verstappen who triumphed. If they were to challenge Mercedes, Red Bull needed Alex Albon to be close to Verstappen's pace but, sadly, he was rarely so.

2020 DRIVERS & RESULTS

Driver	Nationality	Races	Wins	Pts	Pos
Max Verstappen	Dutch	17	2	214	3rd
Alex Albon	British/Thai	17	0	105	7th

FOR THE RECORD

Country of origin:	**England**
Team base:	**Milton Keynes, England**
Telephone:	**(44) 01908 279700**
Website:	**www.redbullracing.com**
Active in Formula One:	**As Stewart GP 1997-99, Jaguar Racing 2000-04, Red Bull Racing 2005-2021**
Grands Prix contested:	**438**
Wins:	**64**
Pole positions:	**63**
Fastest laps:	**68**

THE TEAM

Chairman:	**Dietrich Mateschitz**
Team principal:	**Christian Horner**
Chief technical officer:	**Adrian Newey**
Technical director:	**Pierre Wache**
Chief engineering officer:	**Rob Marshall**
Chief engineer, aerodynamics:	**Dan Fallows**
Chief engineer, car engineering:	**Paul Monaghan**
Team manager:	**Jonathan Wheatley**
Chief engineer:	**Guillaume Roquelin**
Test driver:	**Alex Albon**
Chassis:	**Red Bull RB17**
Engine:	**Honda V6**
Tyres:	**Pirelli**

in F1, namely the automotive company trying to be involved with the day-to-day running of the team and this led to obstruction and frustration.

For 2005, though, that was no longer a factor as the team was sold to the co-founder of the Red Bull energy drink company, Dietrich Mateschitz, and the management was allowed to get on with its business without interference again. Immediately, with its dark blue cars topped by a giant charging red bull, the team gained support for looking distinctive. Progress on the track didn't come immediately, but once Adrian Newey was coaxed across from McLaren in the wake of David Coulthard's signing, the wins started to flow. And the titles too, with Sebastian Vettel heading a four-year run of success from 2010 to 2013, ably supported by Webber.

Red Bull Racing is principally a promotional tool for the company's energy drinks and it fitted in well with Red Bull's image fostered by its support of extreme action sports. Its hospitality facility in the paddock is one of the places to be and be seen, imbued with a rebellious presence in an often serious and corporate air.

Since then, Red Bull Racing has always been in the hunt, but outflanked by Mercedes and Ferrari's facilities, with their ample budgets to spend that bit more to stay ahead. Engines have also been an issue, as Mercedes and latterly Ferrari have had the best engines, and Red Bull has had to make do with engines from Renault, with which it fell out, then Honda, leaving them almost aiming for podium finishes rather than wins. That said, Max Verstappen has given the team something very special since being promoted in 2016 from Red Bull's junior team – Scuderia Toro Rosso as it was then, but now AlphaTauri – and winning first time out. The Dutch ace added two more wins in 2017, two in 2018, three in 2019 and two in 2020, giving the definite impression that he never gives anything less than everything.

Alex Albon has been impressive too since being promoted from Toro Rosso midway through 2019, emphasizing how Dietrich's right-hand man Helmut Marko isn't afraid to keep Red Bull's many scholarship drivers on their toes by promoting and demoting them without mercy. For those losing their ride with Red Bull it can be career ending, although Pierre Gasly bounced back from his demotion to Toro Rosso in 2019 by finishing second at Interlagos and then going one better to win for AlphaTauri at Monza last year.

"Honda's decision to withdraw from F1 presents obvious challenges for us as a team, but we have been here before and with our strength in depth are well prepared and equipped to respond effectively."

Christian Horner

Jackie and Paul Stewart congratulate Rubens Barrichello on second place at Monaco in 1997.

17

MAX VERSTAPPEN

Give Max a car and he will extract the maximum from it. That his Honda-powered Red Bull hasn't been able to live with the pace of the Mercedes for the past few years has been a disappointment, but he never stops trying.

Max demonstrated resilience in 2020, but will pounce when Mercedes blinks.

Max has racing blood in his veins as not only was his father Jos an F1 star but his mother Sophie (Kumpen) was a top kart racer too. His list of karting titles is testament to his talent, from the Belgian Rotax Minimax crown at the age of nine to the World and European titles he claimed seven years later in 2013.

Then came car racing, and you had to blink or you would have missed Max's passage to F1. Such was his pedigree that it was decided to head directly to F3 in 2014. More than that, all of his transition was going to be done on the competitive stage of the European series. Typically, Max didn't hang around and was a race winner by the sixth race, before adding nine more for van Amersfoort Racing to rank third overall as Esteban Ocon took the crown.

Not seeing any reason to bother with GP2, he was signed by Scuderia Toro Rosso for 2015 and became F1's youngest ever starter at the age of 17 after just that one year of car racing.

Max was more than ready for F1, as he came seventh in his second race then fourth in Hungary and again at COTA. His 2016 season took a sudden turn for the better when, after four rounds, he was promoted to Red Bull Racing, with Daniil Kvyat being demoted to make way. Stunningly, he won on his debut in Spain, naturally becoming F1's youngest ever winner.

Max has remained with Red Bull Racing ever since and, at the age of 23, he feels like one of F1's veterans. He has done all that has been asked of him, won ten grands prix and ranked as the best of the best behind the Mercedes drivers in 2019 and 2020. What all fans would like to see is how he would rank against Lewis Hamilton if they were given equal machinery.

TRACK NOTES

Nationality:	**DUTCH**
Born:	**30 SEPTEMBER 1997,**
	HASSELT, BELGIUM
Website:	**www.verstappen.nl**
Teams:	**TORO ROSSO 2015-16,**
	RED BULL RACING 2016-21

CAREER RECORD

First Grand Prix: **2015 AUSTRALIAN GP**
Grand Prix starts: **119**
Grand Prix wins: **10**
2016 Spanish GP, 2017 Malaysian GP, Mexican GP, 2018 Austrian GP, Mexican GP, 2019 Austrian GP, German GP, Brazilian GP, 2020 70th Anniversary GP, Abu Dhabi GP
Poles: **3**
Fastest laps: **10**
Points: **1162**
Honours: **2013 WORLD & EUROPEAN KZ KART CHAMPION, 2012 WSK MASTER SERIES KF2 CHAMPION, 2011 WSK EURO SERIES CHAMPION, 2009 BELGIAN KF5 CHAMPION, 2008 DUTCH CADET KART CHAMPION, 2007 & 2008 DUTCH MINIMAX CHAMPION, 2006 BELGIAN ROTAX MINIMAX CHAMPION**

MORE PODIUMS, BUT FEWER RACE WINS

A power unit failure in the opening grand prix of the season in Austria can't have filled Max with hope for the season ahead, but he bounced back and was invariably the driver who came closest to toppling the dominant Mercedes duo. This was made easier in 2020 than it had been in 2019, as the Ferrari challenge was severely dented without the power advantage that they had once enjoyed. This left Max looking to extract the most performance he could from his Honda-engined RB16, and he had reason to be pleased when he finished ahead of Valtteri Bottas both in the Hungarian and British GPs, although he will regret a late-race precautionary tyre-change in the latter as it cost him victory. Then, at the fifth round, he took that breakthrough win. This was in the 70th Anniversary GP at Silverstone, and he had his team to thank for its superior strategy on Pirelli's softer rubber as he finished 12s clear of Hamilton. Retirements at Monza, Mugello and Imola hurt his hopes of moving ahead of Bottas but he finished on a high with victory in Abu Dhabi.

SERGIO PEREZ

It seemed extraordinary as the end of last season approached that Sergio was heading for the sidelines after being replaced by Sebastian Vettel for 2021, especially when he won the Sakhir GP. However, sense prevailed and he was signed by Red Bull.

Sergio has landed on his feet at Red Bull, and will look to add to his maiden GP win.

Sergio had an important talent that didn't really show itself during his time in the junior single-seater formulae, but has become crystal-clear since he reached F1: he knows how to be really light on his tyres. This ability is an engineer's dream, as it provides infinitely more scope for them to adapt a strategy as a race runs its course or conditions change. On some occasions, it can be even more advantageous than that final 0.1s per lap of ultimate speed.

Like all his rivals, Sergio spent his school years racing karts alongside his studies. Eventually, racing won out, and by the time Sergio turned 14 his family agreed that he could head north over the border from his native Mexico to try single-seaters in the USA. He started in the Skip Barber series and showed enough pace in this to be shipped off to Europe in 2005, where he ranked sixth in his second year in the German Formula BMW series.

For 2007, aged 17, he moved on to British F3, racing in the lesser National class. A year later, he went for the overall title and won four times, but ended up fourth overall.

It was surprising, given his ability to preserve tyre life, that the more powerful GP2 cars suited Sergio better, but he came on strong to rank second in his second season, enough to land him his F1 break with Sauber, assisted by a healthy batch of Mexican sponsors.

That first year in F1, 2011, was adequate, but the team had a far better car in 2012 and Sergio came close to beating Fernando Alonso's dominant Ferrari in a wet Malaysian GP. This performance, plus two further podiums, earned him a promotion to McLaren for 2013. It was to be a one-year stay though, as he ranked only 11th to Jenson Button's sixth.

Sergio then moved to Force India and there he stayed, even through its name change to Racing Point in 2019, as a mainstay of the team. Last year's ranking of fourth overall outstripped his previous best ranking of seventh in 2016 and 2017.

TRACK NOTES

Nationality:	**MEXICAN**
Born:	**16 JANUARY 1990,**
	GUADALAJARA, MEXICO
Website:	**www.sergioperezf1.com**
Teams:	**SAUBER 2011-12,**
McLAREN 2013, FORCE INDIA 2014-18,	
	RACING POINT 2019-20,
	RED BULL RACING 2021

CAREER RECORD

First Grand Prix:	**2011 BAHRAIN GP**
Grand Prix starts:	**191**
Grand Prix wins:	**1**
	2020 Sakhir GP
Poles:	**0**
Fastest laps:	**4**
Points:	**706**
Honours:	**2010 GP2 RUNNER-UP,**
2007 BRITISH FORMULA THREE NATIONAL	
	CLASS CHAMPION

PROVING HIS WORTH ALL OVER AGAIN

Starting with a pair of sixth-place finishes in the two grands prix held in Austria was a good way to get the season rolling for Sergio. However, there was soon unwanted attention as Racing Point was put under the spotlight. Its RP20s were considered to have brake ducts that looked too similar to the equivalent parts on the 2019 Mercedes F1 W10, getting rival teams to activate their lawyers. As this cleared, there was another early setback, when Sergio had to miss the two grands prix held at Silverstone after being found Covid-19 positive. This cost Sergio momentum, but he was soon back up to speed on his return. From the Tuscan GP onwards, he kept improving, including a great run in the tricky Turkish GP when he and Lewis Hamilton were so light on their intermediates that they were able to avoid making a second pitstop. Sergio claimed the third second place of his career there, and followed up with his first win at Sakhir when a pitstop blunder and a puncture denied George Russell the win for Mercedes.

McLAREN

It's out with Renault engines and in with Mercedes power for 2021 which ought to give the cars extra urgency. With Carlos Sainz Jr having moved to Ferrari, there is much excitement about Lando Norris being joined by Daniel Ricciardo.

Lando Norris produced some great runs last year, notably in Austria, and will have to be on his toes with new team-mate Daniel Ricciardo.

Last year was a landmark year for the team, as it marked the 50th anniversary of the death of founder Bruce McLaren and it reinforced the great man's driving force that gave the team such broad foundations. You can but feel that he would be proud that the McLaren of the 21st century produces much-admired sports cars for the road as well as augmenting its F1 programme by building cars for other areas of racing, shining in GTs and looking to try and win the Le Mans 24 Hours again.

Certainly, things were very different in the early 1960s when Bruce McLaren decided to follow his former Cooper team-mate Jack Brabham's example of building his own cars. A team could comprise just a handful of people, as opposed to the casts of many hundreds now, and Bruce revelled in this as not just a jack of all trades, a racer with an engineer's brain, but also as a motivator of the troops. Esprit de corps was strong

and what gave McLaren the basis to become competitive in F1 was its success in the North American Can Am sports car series where prize money and

the sale of customer cars was enough to finance everything else.

McLaren's first sports racer, the M1A, hit the track in 1964, its first single-seater

KEY PERSONNEL & 2020 ROUND-UP

JAMES KEY

Sponsored through his engineering degree by Lotus, James got his F1 break in 1998 as a data engineer for Jordan. He was promoted to become technical director at just 33 in 2005. Five years later, he moved to Sauber, then on to be technical director at Scuderia Toro Rosso in 2012. When McLaren announced in 2018 that it would be replacing Tim Goss, James filled the post from the start of 2019 and the team has been on an upswing in form ever since.

THE TEAM LEARNS TO SMILE AGAIN, BUT NOT TO WIN

If McLaren took giant strides back towards respectability in 2019, it built on those last year as it fought to be the best of the rest behind Mercedes and Red Bull Racing. A podium position at the opening round, when Lando Norris came on strong to finish third, was a boost and Carlos Sainz Jr went better still at Monza, coming home second, a blink off a win. What stood out was just how much better McLaren was working as a team, and its consistent gathering of points demonstrated just how much progress it has made.

2020 DRIVERS & RESULTS

Driver	Nationality	Races	Wins	Pts	Pos
Carlos Sainz Jr	Spanish	17	0	105	6th
Lando Norris	British	17	0	97	9th

FOR THE RECORD

Country of origin:	England
Team base:	Woking England
Telephone:	(44) 01483 261900
Website:	www.mclaren.com
Active in Formula One:	From 1966
Grands Prix contested:	881
Wins:	181
Pole positions:	154
Fastest laps:	157

THE TEAM

Executive director:	Zak Brown
Chairman:	Paul Walsh
Team principal:	Andreas Seidl
Technical director:	James Key
Racing director:	Andrea Stella
Production director:	Piers Thynne
Chief engineering officer:	Matt Morris
Chief engineer, aerodynamics:	
	Peter Prodromou
Director of design & development:	
	Neil Oatley
Head of design:	Mark Inham
Team manager:	Paul James
Test driver:	tba
Chassis:	McLaren MCL36
Engine:	Mercedes V6
Tyres:	Pirelli

in 1965 and its first F1 car in 1966. By 1968, McLaren was among the ranks of grand prix winners. Then, in June 1970, Bruce crashed when testing at Goodwood and died of his injuries. His trusted lieutenants took over the reins, guided by Teddy Mayer, and Emerson Fittipaldi became McLaren's first World Champion in 1974 as the team took the constructors' title for the first time. Two years later, James Hunt also used a McLaren M23 to become World Champion.

Then the team failed to keep up as Lotus led the way with ground effect technology and it took a change at the top, with the arrival of Ron Dennis, for McLaren to get back into the hunt. Designer John Barnard produced F1's first carbon fibre monocoque for the MP4 in 1981 and this led the way to a series of cars that set the pace, with Niki Lauda landing the title in 1984, then Alain Prost in 1985 and 1986.

Taking over the Honda engine deal from Williams in 1988 marked the next golden period, with Ayrton Senna joining to claim the 1988 crown before team-mate Prost pipped him in 1989. No other driver could get near them. Then Senna was champion in 1990 and 1991.

By the late 1990s, McLaren had Mercedes engines, Adrian Newey-designed chassis and a driver line-up of Mika Hakkinen and David Coulthard. The Finn was World Champion in 1998 and 1999, but then Ferrari usurped them. It took until 2008 for McLaren be at the top of F1's pile again. After Fernando Alonso and Lewis Hamilton fell agonisingly short in 2007, Hamilton triumphed the following year. But then Brawn GP came up trumps before Red Bull Racing took control. This made Hamilton open to approaches by Mercedes and McLaren hasn't shone as brightly since then. Indeed, losing Mercedes engines after 2015 left it struggling with Honda power. Changing to Renault engines in 2018 at least elevated it to the midfield, but this is not McLaren's natural hunting ground and Andres Seidl's arrival from Porsche in 2018 helped galvanize the team, with clear progress in 2019 and 2020.

With Zak Brown keen to guide McLaren into ever more areas of motorsport, history is on its side, as McLaren won the Le Mans 24 Hours in 1995 at its first attempt, largely thanks to JJ Lehto's pace in the rain. Brown would love to repeat that achievement, or have a McLaren win the Indianapolis 500.

> **"Our results last season, together with the investment in the team by MSP Sports Capital, provide a stable foundation on which we can build towards our goal of getting back to the front of Formula 1."**
>
> Andreas Seidl

James Hunt earned McLaren many fans with his dramatic, season-long title-chase in 1976.

DANIEL RICCIARDO

Having left Red Bull Racing feeling unloved at the end of 2018, Daniel's spell at Renault failed to keep his famous smile on his face until the green shoots of revival were revealed through last year, but joining McLaren might just be what this rapid Australian needs to do just that.

Daniel came on strong with Renault through 2020 and brings good energy to the team.

One of F1's most irrepressible characters, Daniel certainly needed resilience in his early career as his home city of Perth was so far from anywhere and so every race meant considerable travel, even when contesting Australian series. In fact, it was deemed more sensible to contest South-East Asian series as the races were often closer to home.

Daniel did well, placing third in the regional Formula BMW series in 2006. Then, aged 17, he placed fifth in the global Formula BMW finals.

A move to Europe to race in Formula Renault was next – something that was made possible by being signed up for the Red Bull driver scholarship scheme. Their hunch was proved right when he finished as runner-up to Valtteri Bottas in the 2018 European series.

Next stop was the British F3 championship in 2009, and Daniel won that easily for Carlin before graduating to Formula Renault 3.5. He looked at home in that, ending up just short of the title. Looking to go one better in 2011, Daniel's season was transformed halfway through when he was given his F1 break by the tail-end HRT team.

Red Bull money had been behind this elevation and their backing propelled him into one of the seats at Scuderia Toro Rosso for 2012. Daniel didn't waste the opportunity and was moved on up to Red Bull's senior team in 2014. His five years for Red Bull Racing brought his first win in Canada in 2014 and six more before he felt that it was time to move on.

Daniel's move to Renault from Red Bull Racing for 2019 was seen by many as a result of not playing the card in his hand well as he attempted to stand his ground against the team's perceived favouritism towards Max Verstappen. Daniel put on a brave face, but he was unable to match his two wins in 2018 and his best result was fourth place at Monza as he ranked ninth overall, his worst end-of-year position since 2013 when he raced for Toro Rosso and was 14th overall.

TRACK NOTES

Nationality:	**AUSTRALIAN**
Born:	**1 JULY 1989, PERTH, AUSTRALIA**
Website:	**www.danielricciardo.com**
Teams:	**HRT 2011, TORO ROSSO 2012-13, RED BULL RACING 2014-18, RENAULT 2019-20, McLAREN 2021**

CAREER RECORD

First Grand Prix:	**2011 BRITISH GP**
Grand Prix starts:	**188**
Grand Prix wins:	**7**
	2014 Canadian GP, Hungarian GP, Belgian GP, 2016 Malaysian GP, 2017 Azerbaijan GP, 2018 Chinese GP, Monaco GP
Poles:	**3**
Fastest laps:	**15**
Points:	**1159**
Honours:	**2010 FORMULA RENAULT 3.5 RUNNER-UP, 2009 BRITISH FORMULA THREE CHAMPION, 2008 EUROPEAN FORMULA RENAULT RUNNER-UP & WESTERN EUROPEAN FORMULA RENAULT CHAMPION**

COMING GOOD THROUGH THE SEASON

Daniel's second year with the Renault team was much better than his first as the team from Enstone raised its level of competitiveness through the course of the season while some teams trod water and Ferrari in particular lost ground. After having to retire from the opening round with overheating, he then kicked off with a pair of eighth places before it all turned for the better, with fourth place in the British GP, right on the tail of Charles Leclerc's Ferrari. This suggested that a corner had been turned, but was immediately followed by non-scoring finishes at the 70th Anniversary and Spanish GPs. Fortunately, Renault then found a performance improvement relative to its immediate rivals and Daniel produced a string of top-six finishes to propel him up into the upper echelons of the championship top 10. Top results became expected, not just hoped for. Fourth place in Belgium was a turning point, and two third-place finishes gave the team its first podium visits since 2015.

LANDO NORRIS

Lando claimed his first podium finish, impressed with some late-race charges and entertained with some amusing radio messages, but his third year with McLaren needs to be more consistent if his star is to continue to be in the ascendancy.

Lando is all set for a big third year of F1, adding experience to his obvious pace.

Lando was a major noise in kart racing as he raced everything everywhere and gathered titles for fun. These became ever more serious titles as he rose through the levels, with the world KF junior title in 2013 being followed by the senior one in 2014 when he was 14.

With serious money behind him thanks to his father Adam having made a fortune in financial services, Lando was able to burst onto the car racing scene, even getting started at 14 in the Ginetta Junior series which is aimed at young teenagers.

His first exclusive year of car racing, 2015, was frantic as he raced in F4 around Europe and also won the MSA Formula in Britain. His second year was a watershed as Lando had the Midas touch, winning the Toyota Racing Series in New Zealand then returning to Europe to win the European Formula Renault title. He also gained a little F3 experience and ended the year being crowned as the McLaren *Autosport* BRDC young driver.

A full F3 programme was planned for 2017 and Lando really made his name by achieving the rare feat of winning the European title at his first attempt, racing to nine wins for Carlin. He rounded out the year by finishing second in the Macau F3 street race and having his first F1 runs with McLaren

The 2018 F2 season was unusual as the top three drivers were all of the same nationality as Lando fought for honours against fellow British racers George Russell and Alex Albon. They were good friends off the track and this kept the mood light as the competition became ever more intense as the season progressed. In the end, Lando's failure to win more than once left him short of Russell but his consistent point-scoring was enough for him to beat Albon to be runner-up.

Picked to graduate to F1, Lando joined McLaren at the age of 19 in 2019 and a pair of sixth places for a team that was rediscovering its form was a fair return for his first year in the sport's top level.

TRACK NOTES

Nationality:	**BRITISH**
Born:	**13 NOVEMBER 1999,**
	GLASTONBURY, ENGLAND
Website:	**www.landonorris.com**
Teams:	**McLAREN 2019-21**

CAREER RECORD

First Grand Prix:	**2019 Australian GP**
Grand Prix starts:	**38**
Grand Prix wins:	**0 (best result: 3rd, 2020 Austrian GP)**
Poles:	**0**
Fastest laps:	**2**
Points:	**146**
Honours:	**2018 F2 RUNNER-UP, 2017 EUROPEAN F3 CHAMPION, 2016 EUROPEAN FORMULA RENAULT CHAMPION & FORMULA RENAULT NEC CHAMPION & TOYOTA RACING SERIES CHAMPION, 2015 MSA FORMULA CHAMPION, 2014 WORLD KF KART CHAMPION, 2013 WORLD KF JUNIOR KART CHAMPION & EUROPEAN KF KART CHAMPION & KF JUNIOR SUPER CUP WINNER**

RUNNING MUCH CLOSER TO THE FRONT

There were impressive flashes of speed in his maiden season of F1 in 2019, but Lando realized immediately that his second season was going to be very much better when he raced to third place in the opening round in Austria. This was a massive fillip as it heralded McLaren's return to a level of competitiveness at which they could at least aim for podium finishes, if not yet race wins. Fifth place next time out, also at the Red Bull Ring, suggested that all was well and Lando kept on gathering points to spend the middle part of the campaign ranked as high as fourth in the championship. This was impressive, and looked better still as his appreciably more experienced team-mate Carlos Sainz Jr was only 11th at the midpoint. However, the second half of the season will have proven a useful lesson in maintaining performances, as the Spaniard bounced back to eventually overtake Lando.

ASTON MARTIN F1 TEAM

The team that was known as Racing Point until last year now turns out as Aston Martin F1 Team, with multiple World Champion Sebastian Vettel moving across from Ferrari to join Aston Martin shareholder Lawrence Stroll's son Lance.

There will still be flashes of BWT pink on the team's cars in 2021, but they will race as Aston Martins for the first time in F1 since 1960.

It's a case of new season, new name again for this team from opposite Silverstone's main gates. By being rebadged as Aston Martin F1 Team, the outfit that broke into F1 as Jordan in 1991 has its sixth identity. Do try to keep up...

Breaking into F1 has always been a big deal, but it's safe to say that Eddie Jordan didn't have to find as much money comparatively in 1991 to prepare for the leap from running a team in F3000 as he would today. With 18 teams on the grid that year, compared to 10 now, success was far from likely, but Jordan's gorgeous bright green cars made a real impression, ranking fifth overall.

The second year was tougher as a financially beneficial deal to run Yamaha engines left it less competitive. This was pretty much the story for Jordan as it struggled constantly to keep paying the huge bills necessary to take on the top teams. However, Jordan established a modus operandi and has over-performed

ever since, following the mantra of keeping itself mean and keen.

Rubens Barrichello and Eddie Irvine shone for the team in the mid-1990s, even

sharing a podium with Ferrari's Jean Alesi in Canada in 1995. This two-three finish was improved upon at Spa-Francorchamps in 1998 when Damon Hill won a wet/dry

KEY PERSONNEL & 2020 ROUND-UP

OTMAR SZAFNAUER

An electrical engineer who was born in Romania but brought up in the USA, Otmar joined Ford and made his move into F1 when British American Racing broke cover in 1999, appointed as the new team's operations director. He's nothing if not loyal, staying with the team through the rebranding as Honda in 2006, before leaving to join what was then Force India – now Aston Martin – in 2009. As team principal, he was the hand on the tiller under the flamboyant Vijay Mallya before the calmer days as Racing Point.

COMING ON STRONG THROUGH CONTROVERSY

This team from Silverstone has always punched above its weight. Last year, the old Renault team made accusations that Racing Point's cars contained parts that looked to have been copied from the 2019 Mercedes F1 W10. Whether they were or weren't copies, suddenly the Mercedes-powered RP20s were far nearer the front than usual, with Lance Stroll claiming third place in the Italian and Bahrain GPs and Sergio Perez claiming victory in the Sakhir GP.

2020 DRIVERS & RESULTS

Driver	Nationality	Races	Wins	Pts	Pos
Sergio Perez	Mexican	15	1	125	4th
Lance Stroll	Canadian	16	0	75	11th
Nico Hulkenberg	German	3	0	10	15th

FOR THE RECORD

Country of origin:	**England**
Team base:	**Silverstone, England**
Telephone:	**(44) 01327 850800**
Website:	**www.astonmartinf1.com**
Active in Formula One:	**As Jordan 1991-2004, Midland 2005-06, Spyker 2007, Force India 2008-18, Racing Point 2019-20, Aston Martin 2021**
Grands Prix contested:	**535**
Wins:	**5**
Pole positions:	**4**
Fastest laps:	**7**

THE TEAM

Team principal:	**Otmar Szafnauer**
Technical director:	**Andrew Green**
Sporting director:	**Andy Stevenson**
Production director:	**Bob Halliwell**
Chief designers:	**Akio Haga & Ian Hall**
Aerodynamics director:	**Simon Phillips**
Performance engineering director:	**Tom McCullough**
Operations manager:	**Mark Gray**
Test driver:	**tba**
Chassis:	**Aston Martin 2021**
Engine:	**Mercedes V6**
Tyres:	**Pirelli**

race from team-mate Ralf Schumacher. Cue massively enthusiastic celebration. At last, flamboyant Eddie Jordan could walk the walk as well as talk the talk and F1's challenger team had lived up to its promise. Things went even better in 1999 when Heinz-Harald Frentzen won twice and the team ranked third. In 2003, in a soaking Brazilian GP interrupted five times by safety car interventions, Giancarlo Fisichella took a surprise win in a year that yielded little else.

That, though, was as good as it got, as Jordan simply didn't have the funds to topple Ferrari and McLaren. By the end of 2004, Eddie sold up to Alex Shnaider who renamed the team as Midland. That didn't last, so revived Dutch sports car manufacturer Spyker put its name on the cars' noses in 2007. Then the cars were painted in India's colours of white, orange and green in 2008 as drinks industry tycoon Vijay Mallya brought a bigger pot of money. Racing as Force India, the team put up some great performances to showcase the talents of Fisichella – who nearly won the 2009 Belgian GP – Sergio Perez and Paul di Resta, but Mallya was wanted by the Indian authorities for financial irregularities and bills went unpaid for too long, leaving the crew feeling less than secure. Impressively, they kept their focus on the racing, even being classified fourth overall through the best efforts of Perez and Nico Hulkenberg in 2016, but it was extremely unsettling for all concerned. For sheer entertainment, though, the soap opera of intra-team battling between Perez and Esteban Ocon made excellent viewing as they scrapped with each other rather than their rivals in their quest for supremacy.

Cue another name change, and Racing Point became the name on the entry list in 2019 and 2020 after Lawrence Stroll settled the team's debts and took control. More recently, Stroll led a consortium that brought much needed investment to Aston Martin last year, and the team's new-for-2022 base will house Aston Martin's road car design group.

Hopefully, the Aston Martin F1 Team will have considerably more success than when the company dabbled with F1 in 1959 and 1960 and was behind the curve. The DBR4 was outmoded at inception as it had the engine in the front rather than behind the driver like in the nimble Coopers. These Coopers set new standards in what was a British revolution that reinvented F1. The only continuity will be the team's green livery.

Michael Schumacher made his F1 debut for Jordan in Belgium in its first season in 1991.

> **"Sebastian is a proven champion and brings a winning mentality that matches our own ambitions for the future as Aston Martin F1 Team. He will play a significant role in taking this team to the next level."**
>
> Otmar Szafnauer

SEBASTIAN VETTEL

Ferrari fell out of love with this four-time World Champion last year and put all its clout behind the driver that it reckoned would bring in the wins, Charles Leclerc. So, for 2021, Sebastian has moved on to Aston Martin.

Sebastian needs a new environment after a hard time at Ferrari and this might be it.

Sebastian was one of motor racing's golden children, gathering trophies as he pleased. This started in karting when he won German and European titles before stepping up to single-seaters in 2003.

A race winner in his first year in Formula BMW, he won all but two of the 20 races at his second attempt. The European F3 series was another two-year project financed by his Red Bull driver scholarship and, after being top rookie in 2005 when Lewis Hamilton dominated, he ended up second in 2006 behind Paul di Resta.

Alongside this, he tried Formula Renault 3.5 and won one of his three outings in this more powerful category, thus choosing it for 2007. He began the year solidly and did enough for him to break into F1 midway through the year when Robert Kubica was injured. Eighth place on his debut was impressive for the 20-year-old, and he was then slotted in at Scuderia Toro Rosso when it dropped Scott Speed. Fourth place in the Chinese GP cemented his place.

In 2008, Sebastian caused a shock when he qualified on pole at Monza and then an even larger one when he won. Promotion to Red Bull Racing for 2009 heralded more wins and he claimed his first F1 title in 2010, followed by three more before leaving to join Ferrari in 2015.

For perhaps the first time in his career, his performance came into question in 2019 when Charles Leclerc eclipsed him and Sebastian started doing something not seen before, making a run of errors. The end of his time with Ferrari was now being considered, and it would come.

TRACK NOTES

Nationality:	**GERMAN**
Born:	**3 JULY 1987,**
	HEPPENHEIM, GERMANY
Website:	**www.sebastianvettel.de**
Teams:	**BMW SAUBER 2007,**
	TORO ROSSO 2007-08, RED BULL
	RACING 2009-14, FERRARI 2015-20,
	ASTON MARTIN 2021

CAREER RECORD

First Grand Prix:	**2007 UNITED**
	STATES GP
Grand Prix starts:	**258**
Grand Prix wins:	**53**

2008 Italian GP, 2009 Chinese GP, British GP, Japanese GP, Abu Dhabi GP, 2010 Malaysian GP, European GP, Japanese GP, Brazilian GP, Abu Dhabi GP, 2011 Australian GP, Malaysian GP, Turkish GP, Spanish GP, Monaco GP, European GP, Belgian GP, Italian GP, Singapore GP, Korean GP, Indian GP, 2012 Bahrain GP, Singapore GP, Japanese GP, Korean GP, Indian GP, 2013 Malaysian GP, Bahrain GP, Canadian GP, German GP, Belgian GP, Italian GP, Singapore GP, Korean GP, Japanese GP, Indian GP, Abu Dhabi GP, United States GP, Brazilian GP, 2015 Malaysian GP, Hungarian GP, Singapore GP, 2017 Australian GP, Bahrain GP, Monaco GP, Hungarian GP, Brazilian GP, 2018 Australian GP, Bahrain GP, Canadian GP, British GP, Belgian GP, 2019 Singapore GP

Poles:	**57**
Fastest laps:	**38**
Points:	**3018**

Honours: **2010, 2011, 2012 & 2013 F1 WORLD CHAMPION, 2009, 2017 & 2018 FORMULA ONE RUNNER-UP, 2006 EUROPEAN FORMULA THREE RUNNER-UP, 2004 GERMAN FORMULA BMW ADAC CHAMPION, 2003 GERMAN FORMULA BMW ADAC RUNNER-UP, 2001 EUROPEAN & GERMAN JUNIOR KART CHAMPION**

FALLING FROM GRACE AT FERRARI

There was a time when it was inconceivable that Sebastian would be forced to leave a team before he wanted to, as this driver who had four F1 titles to his name by the age of 26 was once the pick of the pack. Yet, seven years on, he was eased towards the door by Ferrari. Looking back at his record in karts and then car racing, it's all the more perplexing, as he has never been anything other than the among fastest of the fast, but whether it was the politics at Ferrari or the realization that he was driving a car that could no longer even get close to the Mercedes that wore him down is a moot point. Whatever, he was at sea in 2020, often qualifying outside the top 10 and only infrequently finishing in it. When team-mate Leclerc came second in the opening round and Sebastian was 10th, that seemed to set the tone, and as Ferrari struggled so he "said things that perhaps he should not have". To end the year with a third place finish in the Turkish GP as his best result was a shock.

LANCE STROLL

Last year was the year that Lance came of age in F1 with a string of strong results as Racing Point hit great form. This year, at the rebranded Aston Martin, he has a new driver to compare himself against: Sebastian Vettel.

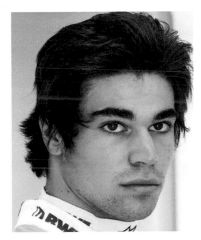

Lance peaked with third place at Monza and so might fancy his chances against Vettel.

Clearly, there are more sons and daughters of millionaires racing karts and cars than there are those of people of more modest means, but Lance had extra push to his career as his father Lawrence isn't just a car and racing fanatic but a billionaire rather than a mere millionaire.

As a consequence, Lance wanted for nothing as he spread his wings in karting, bagging local titles before spending time racing in Italy. Then, in 2013, aged 14, he finished fifth in the world kart championship, earning selection for Ferrari's driver academy. That was a good fit for his father, who raced Ferraris.

When he was 15, his father was happy to put him into car racing, starting with a Ferrari-backed series based in Florida. Lance demonstrated obvious natural speed and so spent the year contesting the Italian F4 series, winning that.

Anxious to gain experience as quickly as possible, Lance then spent the winter of 2014-2015 contesting the New Zealand-based Toyota Racing Series, winning that as well.

Next stop was F3 in 2015 and Lance was very quick but flawed, having a string of accidents in his pursuit of success in the European championship. A second year in European F3 was considered wise and Lance smashed it, winning almost half of the 30 races.

With his father an investor in Williams, he was given his first taste of F1 and did well. Williams then offered him a ride for 2017, meaning that he was 18 when he reached F1, but he wasn't overawed and scored 40 points to veteran team-mate Felipe Massa's 43, peaking with a surprise third in the Azerbaijan GP.

His second year with Williams was much harder as the team's performance plummeted in 2018, so he moved teams for 2019 after his father was part of the consortium that saved Force India and gave it its new name.

Trying to match the pace of established team leader Sergio Perez has been Lance's main challenge since then, with fourth place at Hockenheim his best result in 2019 before he went better still last year.

A YEAR OF MATURITY AND NEW PACE

It was clear from the delayed opening race of last year that the Racing Point team was going to be racing closer to the front of the field in 2020 than it had been in 2019. This thrilled Lance and team-mate Sergio Perez, and they set about recording top-six results for fun, powering Racing Point to fourth place in the constructors' table by the middle of the season, three places higher than in 2019. Fourth place in the Hungarian GP was a fillip, but clearly no fluke as Lance claimed a similar result three races later in Spain. Then, he equalled his previous best finish by coming third at Monza, and he was heading for fourth place the following weekend at Mugello until a suspected puncture sent him into the barriers. This was a setback, then there was another non-score next time out, in Russia, and then he missed the Eifel GP with a Covid scare, but Lance was by now treated as the team's lead driver and he made the most of being the first to receive upgrades as they were introduced, peaking with third at the Sakhir GP.

TRACK NOTES

Nationality:	**CANADIAN**
Born:	**29 OCTOBER 1998, MONTREAL, CANADA**
Website:	**www.lancestroll.com**
Teams:	**WILLIAMS 2017-18, RACING POINT 2019-20, ASTON MARTIN 2021**

CAREER RECORD

First Grand Prix:	**2017 AUSTRALIAN GP**
Grand Prix starts:	**78**
Grand Prix wins:	**0 (best result: 3rd, 2017 Azerbaijan GP, 2020 Italian GP, Sakhir GP)**
Poles:	**1**
Fastest laps:	**0**
Points:	**142**
Honours:	**2016 FIA EUROPEAN FORMULA THREE CHAMPION, 2015 TOYOTA RACING SERIES CHAMPION, 2014 ITALIAN FORMULA FOUR CHAMPION**

Lance Stroll impressed for Racing Point. This year the car will race in Aston Martin green.

» ALPINE

A fresh new season stands ahead after this team's fifth name change since it hit F1 as Toleman back in 1981. The Renault engines remain, but the team name has changed from Renault to Alpine as Fernando Alonso returns to lead its attack.

Esteban Ocon will be out to prove that he has the pace to stand up to the challenge of returning team favourite and champion Fernando Alonso.

The order goes like this: Toleman, Benetton, Renault, Lotus then Renault again. This isn't a sequence of cars in a race but the names under which this team has operated since breaking into the World Championship in 1981. To add to the confusion as teams change names, the Renault and Lotus teams listed were not the original works teams that carried those names. Then, in a change announced at last year's Tuscan GP by Renault's new CEO Luca de Meo, it has been renamed as Alpine after Renault's sports car brand that has competed successfully in rallying and more recently endurance racing. The team livery changed from black and yellow to French blue.

Transport magnate Ted Toleman built a team that shone in F2. When it stepped up to F1 in 1981, its cars seldom qualified as Williams, Brabham and the works Renault teams set the pace. By 1984, though, with rookie Ayrton Senna at the wheel, the team came within a blink of winning in Monaco.

The team was rebadged as Benetton in 1986, in deference to the Italian knitwear company. The multi-coloured cars were spectacular in qualifying with their flame-spitting BMW turbo engines, but suffered many retirements until Gerhard Berger won in Mexico. The loss of BMW engines for 1987 was seen as a

KEY PERSONNEL & 2020 ROUND-UP

PAT FRY
Despite having started his career working on missiles, Pat turned to racing in 1987, working on Benetton's active suspension before becoming Martin Brundle's race engineer. Following former colleague Giorgio Ascanelli to McLaren in 1993, he became race engineer for Mika Hakkinen then David Coulthard. After taking on ever greater responsibility, he joined Ferrari in 2010 as assistant technical director. Internal changes forced him to quit in late 2014, moving first to Manor, then to McLaren as a stand-in engineering director. He joined Renault for 2020.

GOOD RACE PACE IS BEGINNING TO RETURN
The team's final year as Renault began with Daniel Ricciardo and Esteban Ocon in the lower reaches of the top 10, but improvement followed and Ricciardo began to feel podium finishes were possible as he collected a string of fourths. Then came the news midseason that the team would run under the Alpine name from 2021 and there's belief that this new identity will mark a further boost in its level of competitiveness, especially with Fernando Alonso returning.

2020 DRIVERS & RESULTS

Driver	Nationality	Races	Wins	Pts	Pos
Daniel Ricciardo	Australian	17	0	119	5th
Esteban Ocon	French	17	0	62	12th

FOR THE RECORD

Country of origin:	England
Team base:	Enstone, England
Telephone:	(44) 01608 678000
Website:	www.renaultsport.com
Active in Formula One:	As Toleman 1981-85, Benetton 1986-2001, Renault 2002-11 & 2016-2020, Lotus 2012-15, Alpine 2021
Grands Prix contested:	672
Wins:	48
Pole positions:	34
Fastest laps:	56

THE TEAM

Chief Executive Officer:	Luca De Meo
Managing director:	Cyril Abiteboul
Executive director:	Marcin Budkowski
Chassis technical director:	Pat Fry
Engine technical director:	Remi Taffin
Chief aerodynamicist:	Dirk de Beer
Sporting director:	Alan Permane
Operations director:	Rob White
Chief engineer:	Ciaron Pilbeam
Team manager:	Paul Seaby
Test drivers:	tba
Chassis:	Renault RS21
Engine:	Renault V6
Tyres:	Pirelli

blow, but Thierry Boutsen was a frequent podium visitor with Ford power in 1988 to help Benetton rank third. Then in 1989 Alessandro Nannini added another win in Japan before Nelson Piquet won the last two races in 1990 to help Benetton back to third.

The biggest breakthrough was snatching Michael Schumacher from Jordan. That was at the end of 1991. A year later, he was a winner. By 1994, he was World Champion. With Ford engines replaced by Renault power in 1995, Schumacher was champion again, as Benetton took its first constructors' crown. Gradually, with Williams assuming control before Ferrari hit the front in 2000, Benetton lost engine deals and so lost ground. Then, in 2001, Renault bought the team and ran it from Benetton's Enstone base under its own name from 2002.

The way to victory was rediscovered in 2003 when Fernando Alonso triumphed in Hungary. He then won world titles with Renault in 2005 and 2006 under the guidance of Pat Symonds, who had been a backbone for the team since its Toleman days, echoing how this team values keeping a stable technical team.

The loss of Alonso to McLaren for 2007 cost momentum, as shown by the team's fall to eighth in 2009 even with Alonso back on board. To make matters worse, Renault was then charged with fixing the result of the 2008 Singapore GP and this led to front man Flavio Briatore and Symonds having to stand down. Luckily, things went better in 2010, with Robert Kubica giving the team hope before he suffered terrible arm injuries that prevented him returning in 2011. Also in 2011, the Lotus Group struck a deal for the team to be entered as Lotus Renault GP. This was rather a strange deal as there was no connection with the works Lotus team of old

Money was a problem, though, and so the team went racing in 2012 with the cars badged as Lotus cars. More exciting was the coaxing of Kimi Raikkonen back from rallying and he won in Abu Dhabi to help the team rank fourth, a level it maintained in 2013 when he won in Australia. Then he left and the team fell from the pace again, even with Mercedes engines.

The team became Renault again in 2016, with the manufacturer pledging its support for five years to offer much-needed stability. Since then, form has gradually returned as Nico Hulkenberg and Carlos Sainz Jr helped it rank sixth in 2017, then fourth in 2018 before Daniel Ricciardo showed pace in 2019.

"Starting in 2021, we will be racing with the Alpine brand and the car will be in the historical colours of French motor racing with blue and the tricolore. We will be the Frenchies on the grid"

Luca de Meo

When the team started in F1 as Toleman, rookie Ayrton Senna made it a challenger in 1984.

31

» FERNANDO ALONSO

Very few drivers go for a third spell with a team, but the chance to join Renault, now Alpine, after two years out of F1 was too good to miss. This double World Champion has vowed to be less critical than he was with McLaren.

Fernando is back and anxious to bring his experience to bear to drive Alpine forward.

Few karting world champions make it to F1, with many failing to find the backing. However, Fernando was so good from the moment he started car racing that the talent spotters swiftly got his name on a contract and the winning outfit belonged to Renault team boss Flavio Briatore.

This followed Fernando winning the Formula Open by Nissan title ahead of more experienced drivers in his first year and then showing outstanding form in F3000, then F1's feeder formula. He ranked fourth, but the nature of his dominant win at Spa was enough to mark him out.

There was no space at Briatore's team, so he farmed Fernando out to the tailend Minardi team for 2001 so that he could gain valuable F1 racing experience. Then, after a year as Renault's test driver, the way was clear for him finally to race for Renault. Before the year was out, Fernando lived up to his promise and took his first win in the Hungarian GP.

By the end of 2006, he had two titles in the bag, but he elected to move to McLaren for 2007. Scrapping with rookie team-mate Lewis Hamilton hadn't been part of his plan, and nor had missing out on a third title by just a point. So, upset, he moved back to Renault for 2008, but it was a less competitive team.

Fernando joined Ferrari in 2010, but no titles came his way in five years of trying, as Sebastian Vettel left him second in 2010, 2012 and 2013. Then came a four-year spell with McLaren, but it was a team below its best and so he elected to focus on winning the Le Mans 24 Hours instead.

Fernando will be relishing the challenge as he joins Alpine, but he won't need pointing out that his last F1 win was as long ago as early in the 2013 season.

TRACK NOTES

Nationality:	**SPANISH**
Born:	**29 JULY 1981, OVIEDO, SPAIN**
Website:	**www.fernandoalonso.com**
Teams:	**MINARDI 2001, RENAULT 2003-06, McLAREN 2007, RENAULT 2008-09, FERRARI 2010-14, McLAREN 2015-18, ALPINE 2021**

CAREER RECORD

First Grand Prix:	**2001 AUSTRALIAN GP**
Grand Prix starts:	**314**
Grand Prix wins:	**32**

2003 Hungarian GP, 2005 Malaysian GP, Bahrain GP, San Marino GP, European GP, French GP, German GP, Chinese GP, 2006 Bahrain GP, Australian GP, Spanish GP, Monaco GP, British GP, Canadian GP, Japanese GP, 2007 Malaysian GP, Monaco GP, European GP, Italian GP, 2008 Singapore GP, Japanese GP, 2010 Australian GP, German GP, Italian GP, Singapore GP, Korean GP, 2011 Bitish GP, 2012 Malaysian GP, European GP, 2013 Chinese GP, Spanish GP

Poles:	**22**
Fastest laps:	**23**
Points:	**1899**
Honours:	**2019 DAYTONA 24 HOURS WINNER, 2018/2019 WORLD ENDURANCE CHAMPION, 2018 & 2019 LE MANS 24 HOURS WINNER, 2005 & 2006 F1 WORLD CHAMPION, 2010, 2012 & 2013 F1 RUNNER_UP, 1999 FORMULA NISSAN CHAMPION, 1997 ITALIAN & SPANISH KART CHAMPION, 1996 WORLD & SPANISH KART CHAMPION, 1994 & 1995 SPANISH JUNIOR KART CHAMPION**

FROM THE ANDES TO INDIANAPOLIS

With the Covid-19 pandemic delaying so many events last year, Fernando found himself frustrated as he was interrupted in his post-F1 quest to win as many of the world's greatest races as possible. Having won the Le Mans 24 Hours in 2018 and 2019 for Toyota, he wanted to add to that a win in one of the world's other classic events outside F1, the Indianapolis 500, to complete a triple crown alongside his world titles. However, a lack of seat time was a hindrance and success eluded Fernando again as he finished a lap down – 21st of the 25 finishers – as another former F1 racer, Takuma Sato, took his second Indy 500 win. Competing in the Dakar Rally was at least a new challenge for him at the start of the year, giving Fernando plenty of seat time on Chile's unforgiving landscape. Also at the start of the year, Fernando kept race-sharp by competing in the wide range of virtual races, including the mock Le Mans 24 Hours. Before the year was out, his contract to return to F1 was signed.

ESTEBAN OCON

Esteban will have a new yardstick for his performance as he will be partnered by a driver whose pace is undoubted and his desire to make a winning return to F1 is huge: Fernando Alonso. It should be a sparky combination.

Esteban will be looking forward to being in a team with a stronger French identity.

When Pierre Gasly took his surprise win in last year's Italian GP for Scuderia AlphaTauri, it was heralded around France as this made him the country's first F1 winner since Olivier Panis triumphed in Monaco in 1996. For a country that had been accustomed through the 1970s and 1980s to having a host of stars in F1, this span without a win had been agonizing.

As a result of this dearth of F1 success, there was a buzz among French aficionados a decade ago, as there was a gang of its own starring in karting. Esteban was one of these, dicing constantly with Gasly and Anthoine Hubert. Charles Leclerc was often bunched in with them, but he is Monegasque.

They didn't stop their winning when they moved into car racing and Esteban made a big splash by going into Formula Renault in 2012 and ranking third in the European series the following year. What made talent-spotters really check on his progress was what happened in 2014 when he moved up to F3 and immediately landed the European series crown in a year that included Max Verstappen.

GP3 came next and Esteban won that title too. Talent can take you only so far, though, and his family didn't have the small fortune required to compete in GP2, so Esteban took an unusual sidestep by leaving single-seaters to race in the DTM touring car series for Mercedes. It served him well though, as he was now on Mercedes' books and this assisted him to get his F1 break in the second half of

2016 when the Mercedes-engined Manor team dropped Ryo Haryanto and Esteban was put there in his place.

In 2017, Esteban joined Force India where he fought with increasing venom against long-established Sergio Perez, the pair colliding increasingly as Esteban challenged the Mexican's supremacy in the team. A fifth place in the Mexican GP in 2017 was his best result in his two years with the team, but there was no ride for 2019 as Lance Stroll brought welcome finance and so he was shunted into the siding for a year until Renault wanted a French driver for 2020.

TRACK NOTES

Nationality:	**FRENCH**
Born:	**17 SEPTEMBER 1996,**
	EVREUX, FRANCE
Website:	**www.esteban-ocon.com**
Teams:	**MANOR 2016, FORCE INDIA**
2017-18, RENAULT 2020, ALPINE 2021	

CAREER RECORD

First Grand Prix:	**2016 BELGIAN GP**
Grand Prix starts:	**67**
Grand Prix wins:	**0**
(best result: 2nd, 2020 Sakhir GP)	
Poles:	**0**
Fastest laps:	**0**
Points:	**198**
Honours:	**2015 GP3 CHAMPION, 2014 FIA**
EUROPEAN FORMULA THREE CHAMPION	

SOME IMPROVEMENT NEEDED

In truth, rather more might have been expected from Esteban on his return to F1 last year after a season spent on the sidelines. As it was, his return from a diet of simulator work to the race track was solid rather than spectacular, and resulted in him lagging behind the scoring rate of his team-mate Daniel Ricciardo. As the Renault RS20 increasingly found a cutting edge, it was Ricciardo who exploited it better. This will have been a matter of concern to Esteban's supporters, of whom there are many up and down the F1 paddock. Perhaps the RS20 didn't give him the confidence it clearly did to his team-mate, but until the penultimate race, his best finish of fifth in the Belgian GP – equalling his career best – wasn't a match for Ricciardo's two thirds. The car was good enough, but it just didn't really click until the Sakhir GP, when Esteban rose to new heights as Mercedes stumbled and he raced to second. Maybe this will reinforce his push in 2021, so that he can shoot for another podium.

The start of last year was a blur for Daniel Ricciardo before Renault found its form.

FERRARI

Sebastian Vettel caught Ferrari by surprise last spring when he announced that he would be leaving and the team moved quickly to secure the services of Carlos Sainz Jr from McLaren to race alongside team leader Charles Leclerc.

Charles Leclerc is Ferrari's standard bearer again in 2021 and will be optimistic that he can return to winning ways after last year's drought.

No team in F1 has a longer history than Ferrari. Not only has it contested grands prix every year since the start of the World Championship in 1950, but it also stretches back way past that to when Enzo Ferrari turned from racing cars for Alfa Romeo to running its racing division in the 1930s. His next career change led to him forming Scuderia Ferrari in 1946 to build road cars, before opening a racing department in 1948. No team can match this for longevity and Ferrari still means both F1 and some of the world's most desired road-going supercars.

What is fantastic is that the team has always run its cars as Ferraris, all painted red, regardless of take-overs like when it merged with FIAT in 1969. For this, F1 fans should be thankful, because recent changes of identity of the midfield teams have only brought confusion, as heritage is cast aside in the race to the top.

After Alfa Romeo left F1 at the end of 1951, the way was clear for Ferrari

and Alberto Ascari grabbed the title in 1952 and 1953 when F1 was run to F2 regulations. Unable to cope with the arrival of Mercedes in 1954, Ferrari struck

back after it withdrew at the end of 1955, with the team taking over Lancia's D50 design and Juan Manuel Fangio doing the honours. Mike Hawthorn resisted the

KEY PERSONNEL & 2020 ROUND-UP

LAURENT MEKIES

This French mechanical engineer joined Arrows in 2001 but became best known for his 12-year stint at Minardi, becoming chief engineer as it morphed into Scuderia Toro Rosso in 2006, being responsible for its trackside operations. Laurent had a change of focus in 2014 when he joined the FIA as the sport's governing body's safety director and he went on to become F1's deputy race director. The lure of working for a team again drew him to Ferrari in late 2018 and he now acts as its sporting director.

A SEASON TO FORGET FOR F1'S OLDEST TEAM

Even with the delayed start to last season, Ferrari realized that it was not as competitive as it would have liked. Mercedes was easily clear, and Red Bull Racing too. A change of command was instigated at the end of July, but there was no clear upswing in form, with Sebastian Vettel increasingly at sea and even podium visits increasingly beyond Charles Leclerc, as second place in the opening round and third in the fourth became distant memories.

2020 DRIVERS & RESULTS

Driver	Nationality	Races	Wins	Pts	Pos
Charles Leclerc	Monegasque	17	0	98	8th
Sebastian Vettel	German	17	0	33	13th

FOR THE RECORD

Country of origin:	**Italy**
Team base:	**Maranello, Italy**
Telephone:	**(39) 536 949111**
Website:	**www.ferrari.com**
Active in Formula One:	**From 1950**
Grands Prix contested:	**1,008**
Wins:	**237**
Pole positions:	**228**
Fastest laps:	**253**

THE TEAM

CEO:	**John Elkann**
Team principal & technical director:	
	Mattia Binotto
Head of chassis:	**tba**
Head of performance development:	
	Enrico Cardile
Head of power unit:	**Enrico Gualtieri**
Head of aerodynamics:	**Loic Bigois**
Sporting director:	**Laurent Mekies**
Head of race activities:	**Jock Clear**
Operations director:	**Gino Rosato**
Chief race engineer:	**Matteo Togninalli**
Reserve driver:	**Callum Ilott**
Chassis:	**Ferrari SF1001**
Engine:	**Ferrari V6**
Tyres:	**Pirelli**

Vanwall challenge to add another title in 1958.

The British teams were coming, though, with Cooper and Lotus fizzing with new ideas, like placing the engine behind the driver. Fortunately for Ferrari, F1's rules were changed so that engines could be no more than 1,500cc, and Ferrari had the best of those, so scooped the title through Phil Hill in 1961. When British teams dominated, Ferrari largely fell away.

Enzo could be autocratic and this led to him losing most of his racing staff at the end of 1962 when chief engineer Carlo Chiti led a walkout. John Surtees did drag the team to the 1964 title through force of personality, but it would be a long wait to hit the top again.

Another strong personality, Niki Lauda, kicked Ferrari into shape in the mid 1970s, with the help of young team manager Luca di Montezemolo, claiming the title in 1975 and 1977. It would have been a hat trick but for dreadful injuries he suffered in the 1976 German GP. Yet, Enzo was still very much in control and unceremoniously replaced Lauda for 1978, bringing in the flamboyant Gilles Villeneuve to replace him.

Jody Scheckter won the 1979 title, but the remorseless aerodynamic and engineering gains by its rivals Brabham, Williams and McLaren left Ferrari trailing. Indeed, Enzo would never see another Ferrari driver crowned as champion before he died in 1988. In fact, the next one wasn't until 2000 when the partnership between Michael Schumacher, technical chief Ross Brawn and team chief Jean Todt bore fruit.

This was to be the start of a golden age, as Schumacher won the next four titles as well thanks to the excellence of Ferrari's now cosmopolitan leadership. Kimi Raikkonen added Ferrari's most recent title in 2007, pipping McLaren's Fernando Alonso and Lewis Hamilton. Since then, though, Ferrari has had to play second fiddle to Red Bull Racing and Mercedes, despite the best efforts of Sebastian Vettel and the driver who has made himself team leader: Charles Leclerc.

Ferrari continues to hold the predominant position in the World Championship and it has been revealed in recent years how the sport's governing body had allowed it voting rights afforded to no other team, explaining why it has so often blocked moves to make the sport cheaper and thus lose one of its advantages. As the world's most famous team, Ferrari knows F1 would be the poorer without it.

"We had a disappointing season, so we have to turn the page, taking on board what we learned during these difficult times and working nonstop on our 2021 car to make up the performance gap."

Mattia Binotto

Felipe Massa leads Kimi Raikkonen at the 2007 Brazilian GP as the Finn heads to the title.

» CHARLES LECLERC

Last year was disappointing for Charles as Ferrari struggled to keep Mercedes in sight, but this year might be just as much of a letdown as the delay of new technical regulations until 2022 has spiked Ferrari's hopes of getting back on terms.

Charles started last year with a second place but it was all downhill from there.

Some drivers make it all look easy, and certainly Charles' first and second years in F1, with Sauber then Ferrari, made him look to be a star. However, this speed was apparent many years earlier as he worked his way through karts and then the junior single-seater categories.

Guided by his racing driver father Herve, he was the best cadet-level karter in France and then won the Monaco Kart Cup on the streets of his home town when he was 13. That was in 2010. By the time he was 15, Charles was runner-up to Max Verstappen as they fought for World KF kart honours.

Stepping up to Formula Renault in 2014, he showed well at regional level and felt confident enough to move directly to F3 in 2015, ranking fourth in the European series. He then rounded out the year with second place in the Macau F3 street race.

In the same way as other current F1 drivers without an ample budget, like George Russell and Valtteri Bottas, he stepped almost sideways from F3 to GP3 and did what was required by landing the title to keep his career momentum going.

Vitally, his manager Nicolas Todt landed him a Ferrari F1 test and the Scuderia saw enough to convince them to put Charles on their books. This helped him to F2 in 2017 and Charles starred for Prema, by winning seven times en route to the title.

Thus the door to F1 swung open and Ferrari placed Charles at Sauber for a learning year and he drove a Sauber in a way that few have across the decades, qualifying consistently well and peaking with sixth place in Baku.

Ferrari had seen enough and promoted him to the works team for 2019. His impact was almost immediate as only an engine glitch denied him victory on the second race, at Sakhir. This put veteran team-mate Sebastian Vettel in his shade and so it remained for the rest of the season as he won at Spa, then Monza, outscoring Vettel as they ranked fourth and fifth.

TRACK NOTES

Nationality:	**MONEGASQUE**
Born:	**16 OCTOBER 1997, MONTE CARLO, MONACO**
Website:	**www.charles-leclerc.com**
Teams:	**SAUBER 2018, FERRARI 2019-21**

CAREER RECORD

First Grand Prix: **2018 AUSTRALIAN GP**

Grand Prix starts:	59
Grand Prix wins:	2
	2019 Belgian GP, Italian GP
Poles:	7
Fastest laps:	4
Points:	401

Honours: **2017 FIA F2 CHAMPION, 2016 GP3 CHAMPION, 2015 MACAU F3 RUNNER-UP, 2014 FORMULA RENAULT ALPS RUNNER-UP, 2013 WORLD KZ KART RUNNER-UP, 2012 UNDER 18 WORLD KART CHAMPIONSHIP RUNNER-UP & EURO KF KART RUNNER-UP, 2011 ACADEMY TROPHY KART CHAMPION, 2010 JUNIOR MONACO KART CUP CHAMPION, 2009 FRENCH CADET KART CHAMPION**

A YEAR OF FALSE HOPES AND DREAMS

Having finished fourth overall in his first year with Ferrari, Charles would have hoped to go at least one place better as he rejoined battle with Mercedes in 2020. However, after managing to take second place in the opening round when he chased Valtteri Bottas to the chequered flag, cracks soon started to appear in the Ferrari attack. The main problem was a lack of grunt from Ferrari's engine and this made it extra hard work in qualifying and increasingly poor starting positions, sometimes outside the top 10, made the race challenge all the trickier. Indeed, the next nine grands prix comprised a third and fourth in the two races at Silverstone, a sixth and an eighth, plus two non-scoring finishes and three retirements. Keeping in touch with Mercedes in 2019 must have seemed like a distant memory. That one of those retirements came from a mistake Charles made at the start of the Styrian GP and resulted in him clattering into team-mate Vettel didn't help the deflated mood in the team.

CARLOS SAINZ JR

When it became clear that Sebastian Vettel's time at Ferrari was coming to an end, the team lured Carlos from McLaren. However, Ferrari needs to step up its game or he will have made a retrograde move.

A new challenge awaits for Carlos and he will be hoping that Ferrari finds some form.

After an illustrious career in karting, first in Spain and then all over the globe, Carlos peaked with victory in the Monaco Kart Cup and second place in the European KF3 series in 2009. Then, aged 15, he moved up to single-seaters.

Carlos started in Formula BMW, ranking fourth at his first attempt. What made people sit up and pay attention to this son of the multiple World Rally Champion was his second year of car racing, when Carlos finished the European Formula Renault season as runner-up.

Taking his Red Bull backing, Carlos advanced to F3 in 2012 but he didn't step up in the way expected, finishing only sixth in the British series and ninth in the European. His GP3 campaign in 2013 was thus make or break and when Carlos ended the year only 10th it seemed that all momentum had gone from his career as others moved past him.

Yet, showing a dogged determination, Carlos tried Formula Renault 3.5 and this more powerful formula was the answer to his prayers as he grabbed the opportunity and stormed to the title.

Red Bull promoted Carlos to F1 in 2015 with its junior team, Scuderia Toro Rosso. His first year was solid and when, early in 2016, Daniil Kvyat was considered not to be performing sufficiently well and was set to be dropped to Toro Rosso, Carlos must have fancied his chances of going in the opposite direction. History relates that the chance went to team-mate Max Verstappen instead, and that he won first time out.

Carlos ploughed on in 2017 and, perhaps impressed by his fourth place in Singapore, Renault took him in for the final four rounds after dropping Jolyon Palmer. In 2018, he was again consistent, if not as fast as team-mate Nico Hulkenberg.

In 2019, Carlos moved go McLaren, a team that was starting to recover its form and he pipped Pierre Gasly and Alex Albon to rank sixth after a run of ever better finishes, peaking with third in Brazil.

TRACK NOTES

Nationality:	**SPANISH**
Born:	**1 SEPTEMBER 1994, MADRID, SPAIN**
Website:	**www.carlossainzjr.com**
Teams:	**TORO ROSSO 2015-17, RENAULT 2017-18, McLAREN 2019-20, FERRARI 2021**

CAREER RECORD

First Grand Prix: **2015 AUSTRALIAN GP**
Grand Prix starts: **119**
Grand Prix wins: **0 (best result: 2nd, 2020 Italian GP)**
Poles: **0**
Fastest laps: **1**
Points: **372**
Honours: **2014 FORMULA RENAULT 3.5 CHAMPION, 2011 EUROPEAN FORMULA RENAULT RUNNER-UP & NORTHERN EUROPEAN FORMULA RENAULT CHAMPION, 2009 MONACO KART CUP WINNER & EUROPEAN KF3 RUNNER-UP, 2008 ASIA/PACIFIC JUNIOR KART CHAMPION, 2006 MADRID CADET KART CHAMPION**

TAKING A SECOND THEN ENDING WELL

Last year wasn't Carlos's best since reaching F1 in 2015, even though it included his best-ever finish. This was second place in the Italian GP and it was only 0.4s behind surprise winner Pierre Gasly's AlphaTauri. Such was the way that he caught the Frenchman, it was reckoned that Carlos would have needed only one more lap to hit the front, so his celebrations were tinged with a bitter-sweet nature as he considered the maiden win that had escaped him. With every point counting in his battle to win the intra-team tussle with Lando Norris, a power unit fire that prevented him starting at Spa-Francorchamps and then accidents leaving him empty-handed at Mugello and Sochi were major setbacks. By this point, it was already known that he was leaving McLaren for Ferrari and many a query was raised as the Italian team's form seemed to be falling away in front of his eyes. What he needed to restore his mojo was a series of late-season races in which he outscored Norris, and in that he succeeded.

SCUDERIA ALPHATAURI

Scuderia AlphaTauri was all geared up to make a splash last year, with its new name and new livery, but even its most ardent supporter couldn't have predicted that it would spring the surprise of the year and win a grand prix.

Pierre Gasly gave the team its first win since being rebadged as AlphaTauri when he beat all the odds and all the opposition at Monza.

It has been an incredible journey for this team from perennial tailender to comfortable midfielder and very occasional grand prix winner.

It all started when Fiat truck dealer Giancarlo Minardi decided to swap from being an occasional competitor in hillclimbs to running cars in Formula Italia. He changed his team's name from Scuderia del Passatore to Scuderia Everest in 1975, fielding a March in F2. At the start of 1976, the team even fielded a Ferrari in the non-championship International Trophy F1 race at Silverstone.

However, the formation of Minardi in 1980 was the start of something more competitive, with Michele Alboreto winning the F2 round at Misano in 1981. With F2 reaching its conclusion in 1985, Minardi elected to make the leap to F1, signing Pierluigi Martini to spearhead his attack. It's safe to say that success was slow in coming, as the team collected just one point in its first 60 grands prix, but Minardi's perseverance earned the team and its black and yellow cars plenty of admirers and he gave a host of up-and-coming Italian talent their F1 break, including Giancarlo Fisichella and Jarno Trulli, plus a certain Spanish ace, Fernando Alonso.

KEY PERSONNEL & 2020 ROUND-UP

DIETRICH MATESCHITZ
Wealthy individuals have long been attracted to F1 and this Austrian who co-founded the Red Bull energy drink company looked to be the latest in the line. He sponsored Sauber from 1995 but, a decade later, he doubled up to rebrand Jaguar Racing as Red Bull Racing in 2005 and also took over Minardi to be his secondary F1 team, Scuderia Toro Rosso. This was the first team to win, at Monza in 2008. Even with four Sebastian Vettel-led titles for Red Bull Racing from 2010-2013 to quench his thirst, Dietrich remains true to F1.

A YEAR GILDED BY A FAMOUS WIN AT MONZA
Roughly once a decade, F1 produces a surprise, and this little team based in Italy has claimed the two most recent shock results to rock the pitlane, namely winning the Italian GP. The first time was Sebastian Vettel's 2008 victory, then Pierre Gasly stepped up to the mark last year. It was a result that gave the team almost as many points as it had scored in all of 2019, added to by a strong run of top-10 finishes for Gasly and Daniil Kvyat.

2020 DRIVERS & RESULTS

Driver	Nationality	Races	Wins	Pts	Pos
Pierre Gasly	French	17	1	75	10th
Daniil Kvyat	Russian	17	0	32	14th

FOR THE RECORD

Country of origin:	Italy
Team base:	Faenza, Italy
Telephone:	(39) 546 696111
Website:	www.alphatauri.com
Active in Formula One:	As Minardi 1985-2005, Toro Rosso 2006-19, AlphaTauri 2020 onwards
Grands Prix contested:	626
Wins:	2
Pole positions:	1
Fastest laps:	1

THE TEAM

Team owner:	Dietrich Mateschitz
Team principal:	Franz Tost
Technical director:	Jody Egginton
Chief designers:	Paolo Marabini & Mark Tatham
Head of aerodynamics:	Brendan Gilhome
Head of vehicle performance:	Guillaume Dezoteux
Team manager:	Graham Watson
Team co-ordinator:	Michele Andreazza
Chief engineer:	Marco Matassa
Chief race engineer:	Jonathan Eddols
Test driver:	tba
Chassis:	AlphaTauri AT02
Engine:	Honda V6
Tyres:	Pirelli

It was always a struggle to survive as F1 became ever more expensive, the gap between the top teams and those at the tail of the field growing by the year.

By 1994, Minardi had to go into partnership with BMS Scuderia Italia, with Giancarlo becoming the minor shareholder. Further woes followed and it took a deal brokered by F1 chief Bernie Ecclestone to keep the team afloat.

In 1999, cruelly, Luca Badoer was laps away from finishing fourth in the European GP at the Nurburgring, to equal the team's best result, when the gearbox failed.

In 2001, Australian aviation mogul Paul Stoddart bought into the team and he ran it for five years, with a highlight of Mark Webber finishing fifth on his debut in their home race in Melbourne in 2002.

Then, in 2006, with money being poured into the team by Red Bull magnate Dietrich Mateschitz, it became the Austrian's second team, named Scuderia Toro Rosso (Team Red Bull). The team base remained in Faenza, but the team soon changed its spots as it could afford to employ more specialist designers and engineers.

Carrying Mateschitz's Red Bull branding in a similar but mildly different way to the Red Bull Racing cars, the ones from Toro Rosso were seen very much as a training ground for the best of the rising stars from a scholarship scheme overseen for Mateschitz by former F1 racer turned team chief Helmut Marko. The policy was simple: snap up a number of the best drivers in the junior categories, karting even; finance their programmes in Formula Renault, then F3; and see who might shine at the top of the sport. The turnover was high, Marko ruthless, and yet the Toro Rosso programme worked, as the best came out the other end and got promoted to Red Bull Racing.

Take Sebastian Vettel; he entered F1 midway through 2007, and before 2008 was out, he had become a winner, taking victory in the Italian GP. For this still largely Italian team, he couldn't have chosen a better venue for the team's first win. That this was achieved before Red Bull Racing took its first win made the celebrations a little confused. Naturally, this landed Vettel a ride with Red Bull Racing, and so the next batch of young stars got their break at Toro Rosso.

Over the intervening years, stand-out results include Daniil Kvyat's third place in Germany and Pierre Gasly's second place in Brazil in 2019.

The team was given a new identity for 2020, with marketing reasons leading to the team changing its livery to a markedly different grey and white hue and its name to Scuderia AlphaTauri.

"Last year, Scuderia AlphaTauri had a fantastic season, being strong and competitive, scoring 107 points on the constructors' championship, the highest number we've taken, so thanks to the team and to Honda."

Franz Tost

Although only fifth, Paul Stoddart and Mark Webber nipped up to the podium in Australia in 2002.

41

⟫ PIERRE GASLY

This French ace produced the moment of 2020 when he sat on the podium taking in the wonder of winning at Monza for AlphaTauri. Now he must stride on and his string of decent results suggest that he is more than capable of reaping more.

Pierre can't expect another win in 2021, but his name is back up in lights.

Pierre rose through karting with a gang of French stars including Esteban Ocon and Charles Leclerc (if you consider Monegasques to be almost French). He did well and was runner-up in the European KF3 series in 2010. Making the move to car racing was the obvious progression and Pierre did this in 2011. He was immediately on the pace in French F4, ranking third.

The European Formula Renault series proved to be rather more of a challenge at his first attempt, but he came back to land the title in 2013.

Ordinarily, this would have set Pierre up for F3, but he used backing from Red Bull to move one stage higher, to Formula Renault 3.5, losing out only to Carlos Sainz Jr, a driver with considerably more experience.

The next stop, in 2015, was GP2, but this again proved to be a two-year challenge and his four wins were just enough for Pierre to edge out Antonio Giovinazzi.

Careers don't always run straight and true, as Red Bull didn't have a vacancy for him in its F1 entry team, Scuderia Toro Rosso. So, instead, it paid for him to race in Japan in 2017, in Super Formula. This is a series in which the top Japanese drivers remain for years, so he had to learn the tracks and take on rivals who really knew their craft. What impressed was the fact that Pierre won twice to end the year as runner-up.

Before the year was out, though, he had become an F1 driver when Toro Rosso gave him a seat in place of Daniil Kvyat

Pierre's first full season in 2018 peaked with fourth place at the Bahrain GP and so earned him promotion to Red Bull Racing in 2019, but he was outpaced consistently by Max Verstappen and was dropped before the year was out, being replaced by Alex Albon. His head could have gone down, but Pierre's response to demotion was impressive, as he then restored his reputation by racing to a fabulous second place in the Brazilian GP behind his former Red Bull Racing team-mate Verstappen, and so put his name back up in lights.

TRACK NOTES

Nationality:	**FRENCH**
Born:	**7 FEBRUARY 1996, ROUEN, FRANCE**
Website:	**www.pierregasly.com**
Teams:	**TORO ROSSO 2017-18 & 2019, RED BULL RACING 2019, ALPHATAURI 2020-21**

CAREER RECORD

First Grand Prix:	**2017 MALAYSIAN GP**
Grand Prix starts:	**64**
Grand Prix wins:	**1 (2020 Italian GP)**
Poles:	**0**
Fastest laps:	**2**
Points:	**199**
Honours:	**2017 JAPANESE SUPER FORMULA RUNNER-UP, 2016 GP2 CHAMPION, 2014 FORMULA RENAULT 3.5 RUNNER-UP, 2013 EUROPEAN FORMULA RENAULT CHAMPION, 2010 EUROPEAN KF3 KART RUNNER-UP**

WORKING MIRACLES FOR ALPHATAURI

Pierre has always been quick. Just take a look at his career record, peppered with titles and, if occasionally less than that, finishing as runner-up. What he did last year, though, was to seize the moment at his team's home race, the Italian GP at Monza – when leader Lewis Hamilton was penalized for a mistake and then deliver in style. It would have been easy to have slipped up, but he knew that this was a potential gift. There was intense pressure from Carlos Sainz Jr at the end, but he hung on for a dream result, winning by just 0.415s. It was like Sebastian Vettel in 2008 when the same Italian team competed as Scuderia Toro Rosso and the German's career exactly didn't go too badly after that. Pierre also shone, albeit briefly, in the Emilia Romagna GP before clutch failure forced him out. By scoring in more than half of the races in 2020, he proved his worth and was constantly reminding his Red Bull overlords that he was ready for a return to its main team to have another crack at Max Verstappen.

YUKI TSUNODA

Red Bull's desire to land an engine deal for 2022 led to AlphaTauri signing this Japanese F2 star for 2021 as part of a package that potentially opens the way for Red Bull to take over the intellectual rights for Honda's F1 engine.

Yuki ended his 2020 F2 campaign on a high and so arrives in F1 with momentum.

Although he's still not yet 21, Yuki already has two years of racing in Europe under his belt, and this will be a big help as he steps up to F1 into a racing environment that will feel considerably less alien as a result.

Yuki's racing career started in Formula 4 in his native Japan just after his 16th birthday, when he tried a couple of races and ended one of them on the podium.

Armed with the knowledge and confidence that he could be competitive, he came back for a full campaign in 2017, raced to three wins and ended the season third overall.

Japanese racers tend not to be encouraged to make rapid leaps up the single-seater ladder, so Yuki returned for a second full F4 campaign in 2018 and his seven wins edged out Teppei Natori for the title.

Then came the big leap as Yuki used backing from Honda to make the move to Europe, going straight into the FIA F3 championship. This was a significant jump, but Yuki started impressively enough with Jenzer Motorsport as he adjusted to this appreciably higher level of the sport, picking up points here and there.

Cleverly, to help him gain more track time, Yuki also contested the lesser Euroformula Open series, also for F3 cars, and he gained not only extra experience but also the confidence that came with a first win, at Hockenheim. Although he missed two rounds, Yuki was able to finish the season fourth overall.

It was in the second half of the FIA F3 season that things changed, as suddenly Yuki was no longer scrapping at the tail of the top 10 but nailed a second place at Spa-Francorchamps. Moving on to Monza, he followed that impressive showing with a third place finish, and then his first win. This helped Yuki to rank ninth and show that he was ready to advance further.

To keep the momentum going, Yuki spent the northern hemisphere close season contesting New Zealand's Toyota Racing Series, and he ranked fourth in that thanks to a win at Hampton Downs. This set him up for a return to Europe, this time to take a shot at the FIA Formula 2 Championship

ALREADY VERSED IN EUROPEAN WAYS

Having proved his speed on the European F3 scene in 2019, Yuki used his backing from the Honda Formula Dream Project and from Red Bull to step up to the FIA F2 series last year with Carlin and it proved to be a very happy hunting ground as he impressed from the outset. Having a fellow F2 rookie as a team-mate, in Jehan Daruvala, it was always going to be intriguing which would come out on top, especially as the Indian had finished just ahead in F3. The answer to this was soon apparent, and Yuki's first win in the sprint race at Silverstone when a late-race charge took him past Robert Schwartzman and Mick Schumacher. Spa-Francorchamps would again prove to be a happy hunting ground for Yuki as he came away with victory in the feature race, albeit having been second behind Nikita Mazepin at flagfall, but promoted to winner when the Russian was penalized 5s for forcing him off the track. Looking to impress at the end of the season, Yuki then won the opening race at the final round to help him to rank third.

TRACK NOTES

Nationality:	JAPANESE
Born:	11 MAY 2000, KANAGAWA, JAPAN
Website:	www.yukitsunoda.com
Teams:	ALPHATAURI 2021

CAREER RECORD

First Grand Prix:	2021 AUSTRALIAN GP
Grand Prix starts:	0
Grand Prix wins:	0
Poles:	0
Fastest laps:	0
Points:	0
Honours:	2018 JAPANESE F4 CHAMPION

Daniil Kvyat guides his AlphaTauri through one of
F1's key corners, Spa-Francorchamps's Eau Rouge.

» ALFA ROMEO

This Italian-backed, Swiss-based, Ferrari-engined team found itself back among the tailenders last year, and it's hard to see how its form will change in 2021 as there are no rule changes from which it might be able to benefit.

Antonio Giovinazzi became accustomed to life outside the points in 2020, and it's hard to see that changing drastically for the season ahead.

F1 can be confusing at times when one charts through its 71-year history. Take Alfa Romeo, the Italian marque that absolutely dominated the first year of the World Championship in 1950, its dark red 158s often filling the top two or even top three finishing positions. That came to a halt when the team was closed after 1951. There was a second Alfa Romeo works team that ran from 1979 to 1985, albeit without wins and with ever-dwindling pace. Then, in 2019, there was a third episode, except this time it wasn't a works effort and had no connection with the earlier Alfa Romeo teams. Indeed, it didn't even operate out of Italy.

The team that fields Alfa Romeo's third F1 team is in all but name the Sauber team, Peter Sauber's outfit from Hinwil in Switzerland, just branded differently.

Peter started in the sport by competing in hillclimbs in a VW Beetle, but he soon took to the circuits to compete in sports car racing. With a strong engineering background, he soon chose to build his own cars, with excellent results leading to an ever more impressive order book.

Mercedes was interested and offered covert funding as Sauber contested the World Sports-Prototype Championship in the mid-1980s. Then Mercedes came

KEY PERSONNEL & 2020 ROUND-UP

FREDERIC VASSEUR

It seems that this French engineer will be best known for his own successful racing team rather than what he has achieved in F1. Frederic's ASM outfit dominated European F3 from 2004 to 2007, guiding Jamie Green, Lewis Hamilton, Paul di Resta and Romain Grosjean to the title. ASM then advanced to GP2 and was renamed as ART Grand Prix, taking the title first with Nico Rosberg then with Hamilton. Alongside building the Formula E chassis, he moved to F1 with Renault, but he soon took the helm at Sauber.

A TEAM CONTINUING TO GO NOWHERE FAST

There had been high hopes when the cars were rebranded in Alfa Romeo's red and white livery that there would be an upswing in form, but this had failed to happen by the end of the second year in these hues. Even finishing in the top 10 appears to be just out of reach, albeit with Antonio Giovinazzi managing ninth place in the opening race in Austria and then Kimi Raikkonen matching that at Mugello in a race with a notable number of retirements.

46

2020 DRIVERS & RESULTS

Driver	Nationality	Races	Wins	Pts	Pos
Kimi Raikkonen	Finnish	17	0	4	16th
Antonio Giovinazzi	Italian	17	0	4	17th

FOR THE RECORD

Country of origin:	**Switzerland**
Team base:	**Hinwil, Switzerland**
Telephone:	**(41) 44 937 9000**
Website:	**www.sauber-group.com**
Active in Formula One:	**As Sauber**
1993-2018 (as BMW Sauber 2006-2010),	
	Alfa Romeo 2019 on
Grands Prix contested:	**502**
Wins:	**1**
Pole positions:	**1**
Fastest laps:	**5**

THE TEAM

Chairman:	**Pascal Picci**
Team principal:	**Frederic Vasseur**
Technical director:	**Jan Monchaux**
Chief designer:	**Simone Resta**
Head of aerodynamics:	**Nicolas Hennel**
	de Beaupreau
Head of engineering:	**Giampaolo Dall'ara**
Head of track engineering:	**Xevi Pujolar**
Head of aerodynamic development:	
	Mariano Alperin-Bruvera
Head of aerodynamic research:	
	Seamus Mullarkey
Head of vehicle performance:	
	Elliot Dason-Barber
Team manager:	**Beat Zehnder**
Third driver:	**Robert Kubica**
Chassis:	**Alfa Romeo C40**
Engine:	**Ferrari V6**
Tyres:	**Pirelli**

out into the open and gave the team full works backing from 1988, moving from race wins to the title in 1989 when Jean-Louis Schlesser came out top just ahead of Jochen Mass. What followed in 1990 though was even more exciting as Mercedes elected to place young German racing stars alongside the established names, thus adding Michael Schumacher, Heinz-Harald Frentzen and Karl Wendlinger to the mix. They all impressed.

By this point, Sauber had a new ambition, to have a shot at F1. Mercedes was going to lend financial assistance, but then backed out of it, leaving Sauber to go it alone for its debut in 1993. JJ Lehto delivered a fifth place finish on the team's debut in South Africa, but it became harder from there for him and for Wendlinger.

Its Ilmor engines were rebadged as Mercedes in 1994, but hopes of progress in 1995 were shattered when Mercedes took those engines to McLaren instead, leaving Sauber to complete the decade in the midfield at best, doing as well as one might expect a privateer team from Switzerland to do. Indeed, one perennial problem was

recruiting the best technical minds, as few wanted to live outside England's F1 crescent.

Then, in 2001, Sauber moved forward. With Petronas-badged Ferrari engines and a driver line-up of Nick Heidfeld and Kimi Raikkonen, the team ranked fourth overall. That was nothing, though, to what followed, as BMW brought engines and finance to Sauber in 2006 and the team sprang forwards, ranking as runner-up to Ferrari in 2007 thanks to the best efforts of Heidfeld and Robert Kubica. There were still no wins, though, but that was finally sorted in 2008 when Kubica led Heidfeld in a one-two finish in Canada.

The deal with BMW came to an end after 2010, and Sauber has run year-old Ferrari engines since then. Life was becoming increasingly more of a struggle and financial survival became ever more imperative until a Swiss financial buy-out saved it in 2016. This came with a change at the top as Peter Sauber was moved aside and Frederic Vasseur arrived from Renault to be installed as team principal.

A boost came in 2018 with the arrival of rookie Charles Leclerc who put the

team where it hadn't been for years, frequently finishing in the top 10, but he moved on immediately to Ferrari, as part of the deal for running Ferrari engines

In 2019, the Sauber name disappeared and the team was rebranded as Alfa Romeo. In Brazil that year they had a great day as Kimi Raikkonen and Antonio Giovinazzi claimed fourth and fifth places.

"With so many races in so little time in 2020, it was really hard to develop the car, but we did make good steps, testament to the good work in Hinwil and at the tracks."

Frederic Vasseur

Back when the team was BMW Sauber, Robert Kubica raced to victory in the 2008 Canadian GP.

KIMI RAIKKONEN

Kept on for a third year with Alfa Romeo, this Finnish veteran still has a level of skill beyond all but a few in F1, but again sadly not the machinery with which to shine except for in occasional cameo roles like in Portugal last year.

Laid back Kimi is back for more of what he does best: racing under the radar.

Kimi doesn't muck around where racing is concerned. He's quick and straight to the point. This, allied with phenomenal natural pace and feel meant that he was able to have the fastest ever rise from karts to F1. Looking back, it's almost laughable. Then, the fact that he finished sixth on his debut in the 2001 Australian GP makes it even more outrageous.

Having ranked second in the 1998 European Super A kart series, he was clearly a rising star, but none would have predicted after he tried Formula Renault at the end of the following season that he would need just one full season in this junior category before he would be given a chance to get into F1.

The opportunity came when his manager urged Sauber to give him a test, and he was such a natural that the Swiss team signed him for 2001. Before he had concluded his debut year ranked 10th, he had his name on a McLaren contract. His five-year spell with a more competitive team led to the first of nine wins, at Sepang in 2003. Kimi's highlight at McLaren was finishing second to Renault's Fernando Alonso in the 2005 drivers' championship.

One thing that Kimi hated from the outset was doing PR duties and this didn't sit well with McLaren, so he moved to Ferrari in 2007 and promptly landed the title in an extraordinary final round at Interlagos. Wins became less frequent after that and Kimi decided to leave F1 and go to an entirely different environment: the World Rally Championship. Yet F1 was still in his blood and he returned in 2012,

racing for Lotus and not only winning in Abu Dhabi but ranking third. Another win followed in 2013 when he ranked fifth.

Then Kimi returned to Ferrari, but his form fell way as he fell under Sebastian Vettel's shadow, until he won the 2018 United States GP. By then, he had agreed to race for his first F1 team again, albeit under its current name of Alfa Romeo.

TRACK NOTES

Nationality:	**FINNISH**
Born:	**17 OCTOBER 1979, ESPOO, FINLAND**
Website:	**www.kimiraikkonen.com**
Teams:	**SAUBER 2001, McLAREN 2002-06, FERRARI 2007-09, LOTUS 2012-13, FERRARI 2014-18, ALFA ROMEO 2019-21**

CAREER RECORD

First Grand Prix:	**2001 AUSTRALIAN GP**
Grand Prix starts:	**332**
Grand Prix wins:	**21**
	2003 Malaysian GP, 2004 Belgian GP, 2005 Spanish GP, Monaco GP, Canadian GP, Hungarian GP, Turkish GP, Belgian GP, Japanese GP, 2007 Australian GP, French GP, British GP, Belgian GP, Chinese GP, Brazilian GP, 2008 Malaysian GP, Spanish GP, 2009 Belgian GP, 2012 Abu Dhabi GP, 2013 Australian GP, 2018 United States GP
Poles:	**18**
Fastest laps:	**46**
Points:	**1863**
Honours:	**2007 FORMULA ONE WORLD CHAMPION, 2003 & 2005 FORMULA ONE RUNNER-UP, 2000 BRITISH FORMULA RENAULT CHAMPION, 1999 BRITISH FORMULA RENAULT WINTER SERIES CHAMPION, 1998 EUROPEAN SUPER A KART RUNNER-UP, FINNISH & NORDIC KART CHAMPION**

AN AMAZING START IN PORTUGAL

Kimi's opening lap in the Portuguese GP at the Algarve International Circuit showed that this Finnish F1 veteran still had it, rising preposterously from 17th place at the start to seventh, then on up to sixth a corner later, making overtaking look laughably simple. That, in essence, was pure Kimi, all skill and no fuss. Yet, for much of the 2020 season, the Finnish veteran had little to keep himself entertained as the Alfa Romeo C39 was only occasionally able to run in the top 10. Points were out of his reach until he came home in ninth place in the crash-strewn Tuscan GP at Mugello, a change from his usual job of running in those seldom televised scraps at the back of the field. Fortunately, an upswing in form towards the end of the year convinced Alfa Romeo to keep branding the team for a further championship campaign. With no rule changes for 2021, don't expect a leap forward, just more of the same.

ANTONIO GIOVINAZZI

Ferrari is keeping faith with this junior driver it has placed at Alfa Romeo for the past two years, as it has seen enough of his improving ability to keep it interested in him for the future, perhaps even as an Italian driver at another Italian team...

Antonio appears to be making gains with each year in F1 with Alfa Romeo.

Top karting results in his native Italy: tick. Competitive in both the European and world series: tick. So far so standard for Antonio as he rose up through the ranks. What followed wasn't, though, as he headed out east to compete in Formula Pilota China. Success in this oriental single-seater series in 2012 helped Antonio to raise a budget to race in British F3 in 2013 and he raced serendipitously for Double R Racing, a team owned by his now F1 team-mate Kimi Raikkonen. Second place overall in that was good enough for Antonio to try the European F3 series in 2014 and he ranked sixth overall as he learned his home continent's leading circuits. Back for a second crack at the European crown in 2015, Antonio finished the year as runner-up to the more experienced Felix Rosenqvist.

What followed suggested that his career might head in a different direction as he spent the winter sharing a sports-prototype with his F3 team-mate Sean Gelael in the Asian Le Mans Series. However, single-seaters were Antonio's true direction and he moved up to GP2 in 2016 and won five races to push the eventual champion Pierre Gasly all the way to the title.

Ferrari put Antonio onto its books as one of its juniors and he was placed with Sauber as its reserve driver. Then when Pascal Wehrlein hadn't recovered from a back injury he was propelled straight into a race seat for the first two rounds.

There was no seat for 2018, so Antonio continued as Sauber's reserve driver, but he did get to contest the Le Mans 24 Hours.

When Sauber was rebadged as Alfa Romeo for 2019, Antonio got his F1 ride. The season was a slow-burner, but Antonio found improved pace in the second half of the year and he appeared to have peaked with ninth place in his home grand prix, but then came the penultimate round, at Interlagos. He was one of the few not to crash. Next time out, he was 16th, which was far more representative of his season.

TRACK NOTES

Nationality: **ITALIAN**
Born: **14 DECEMBER 1993, MARTINA FRANCA, ITALY**
Website: **www.antoniogiovinazzi.com**
Teams: **SAUBER 2017, ALFA ROMEO 2019-21**

CAREER RECORD

First Grand Prix: **2017 AUSTRALIAN GP**
Grand Prix starts: **40**
Grand Prix wins: **0**
 (best result: 5th, 2019 Brazilian GP)
Poles: **0**
Fastest laps: **0**
Points: **18**
Honours: **2016 GP2 RUNNER-UP, 2015 FORMULA 3 MASTERS WINNER & EUROPEAN FORMULA 3 RUNNER-UP, 2013 BRITISH FORMULA 3 RUNNER-UP, 2012 FORMULA PILOTA CHINA CHAMPION, 2010 & 2011 WSK MASTERS SERIES KF2 KART CHAMPION**

STRAIGHT INTO THE POINTS

Scoring points and racing for the Alfa Romeo team certainly aren't natural bedfellows. So, when Antonio kicked off last year's campaign in Austria with a ninth place, he must have felt that the year ahead might yield more than his 2019 debut season did, save for that shock fifth place in Brazil. There had been numerous retirements in that opening race at the Red Bull Ring though, and his 14th place at the same venue the following weekend in the Styrian GP was more true to what he would expect. The key to Antonio's season was that he raced better than before, and a decent run of 11th, 10th, 15th and 10th in the rounds from Sochi to Imola showed a clear progression as he was close to or even outracing Kimi Raikkonen. This improved form was enough for the team to sign Antonio for a third year and it's up to him to keep gaining experience that might help him open the door to a ride with one of F1's top teams. Having a former Ferrari driver as both team-mate and yardstick has its uses after all.

Looking for an advantage, Romain Grosjean strays beyond the circuit edge in his Haas in 2020.

HAAS F1

Scoring just three points last year marked a new low for F1's American team and it may not be long for the sport as it would be easy for the team to concentrate on its NASCAR programme that is so much more successful.

Kevin Magnussen gave his all in 2020, but the Haas F1 team struggled to score points as its Ferrari engine couldn't match the Mercedes units.

There is a fairly established pattern for teams entering F1. Some start a team in a junior single-seater category, advance up the ranks towards F1 and then make the leap when both the time and the money are alright. Others prefer to simply rebrand a team that's already competing in F1. And then there's Haas F1.

In place of these early steps, machining magnate Gene Haas went stock car racing in his native America, climbing up the NASCAR ranks. By 2014, his Haas-Stewart team was a regular front-running outfit, with Kevin Harvick landing the drivers' title and his Haas Automation brand known across the USA. Inspired by this and looking to repeat this sporting and marketing success on a global basis, Gene Haas elected to create a parallel racing programme to run in F1.

Already this was bucking a trend, as teams that do best in F1 are based in Europe, not North Carolina. Secondly, American teams in F1 have been few and

far between and none notably successful beyond brief peaks. Think Shadow, Parnelli and Penske. There was also the spectre of the aborted attempt for Team USF1 to break into the World Championship in 2010, but Haas was up for the challenge.

Still, having a technical partnership with Ferrari from the outset was a wise move,

KEY PERSONNEL & 2020 ROUND-UP

GUENTHER STEINER

Famed for his direct speaking when his drivers have clashed again, as shown on Netflix's *Drive to Survive* series, this Italian engineer is a very human face in a generally overly serious world. He brings broad experience, having spent years in the World Rally Championship with Mazda, Prodrive and then M-Sport. Guenther's move to F1 came in 2001, with Jaguar Racing, which he left when it changed to Red Bull Racing. He then ran a composites firm in the USA, but was lured back when Gene Haas formed his team.

POINTS PROVE ELUSIVE FOR HAAS F1 IN 2020

Having scored points for fifth place on its F1 debut in 2016, Haas F1 could never have considered that it would become so much less competitive in its fifth year at the sport's top level that it would manage to get into the top 10 on only two occasions. Yet that is what happened last year as both Kevin Magnussen and Romain Grosjean struggled to find pace, not helped by their Ferrari engines no longer matching their rivals' power units.

2020 DRIVERS & RESULTS

Driver	Nationality	Races	Wins	Pts	Pos
Romain Grosjean	French	15	0	2	19th
Kevin Magnussen	Danish	17	0	1	20th
Pietro Fittipaldi	Brazilian	2	0	0	23rd

FOR THE RECORD

Country of origin:	USA
Team bases:	Kannapolis, USA, & Banbury, England
Telephone:	(001) 704 652 4227
Website:	www.haasf1team.com
Active in Formula One:	From 2016
Grands Prix contested:	100
Wins:	0
Pole positions:	0
Fastest laps:	2

THE TEAM

Team owner:	Gene Haas
Team principal:	Guenther Steiner
Chief operating officer:	Joe Custer
Technical director:	Rob Taylor
Vice-president of technology:	Matt Borland
Team manager:	Dave O'Neill
Chief aerodynamicist:	Ben Agathangelou
Group leader aerodynaicist:	Christian Cattaneo
Head of logistics:	Peter Crolla
Chief engineer:	Ayao Komatsu
Test driver:	tba
Chassis:	Haas VF-21
Engine:	Honda V6
Tyres:	Pirelli

53

and an even better one was starting with a chassis designed and built by Dallara rather than electing to do it themselves in-house. This allowed the team to concentrate on its first year operational logistics, including taking the wise decision to operate its season out of a European base. Better still, they chose the former Marussia team base in Banbury, right in the heart of England's F1 crescent of excellence.

So, it was with little expectation of success that the established teams watched on at the start of 2016 and were rocked when Romain Grosjean raced to sixth place on the team's debut in Melbourne. It was a crazy race, though, but then he followed this with fifth place next time out in a more regular affair in Bahrain. Sadly, this spectacular start was to prove a false dawn as he scored on just three more occasions and team-mate Esteban Gutierrez not at all.

In 2017, Haas again ranked eighth out of the 11 teams, ending up not far off Scuderia Toro Rosso's tally as Grosjean scored eight times along with Kevin Magnussen's five point finishes.

Haas F1's third year in F1 was much more like it as it vaulted past Toro Rosso and Force India to rank fifth overall, with Magnussen twice finishing fifth in races to rank ninth overall. Grosjean took the team's best result that year, coming home fourth in the Austrian GP just ahead of Magnussen on a day when neither Mercedes finished.

In 2019, though, Magnussen kicked off with a sixth place finish in Australia but then the team really tumbled to end the year ahead only of hapless Williams with a car that had a fair amount of pace in qualifying but really lost its edge across a race distance. Haas F1 wasn't always a happy camp as all involved grew frustrated at their lack of performance, with team principal Guenther Steiner certainly not holding back in telling drivers Grosjean and Magnussen precisely what he thought of them after they clashed at the British GP to leave both on the sidelines. It wasn't the only time they collided in 2019. Add to this an on/off sponsorship saga with Rich Energy, and the team was fighting battles in which it didn't need to be involved, all taking focus away from the team's continued failure to develop a car across the course of a season, as shown by its failure to score even a single point in the final five rounds.

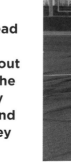

"We are just looking ahead to the 2021 season. We will try our best to get out of the hole we're in at the moment and everybody will put their effort in and I will make sure that they do so."

Guenther Steiner

Romain Grosjean gave Haas a dream start in F1 in 2016 when he finished sixth in Australia.

NIKITA MAZEPIN

This 22-year-old son of a Russian billionaire scored a couple of F2 wins last year but he has been given his F1 break chiefly because of the Haas team's need for financial input at a time when several F1 teams are struggling.

Nikita made a social media gaffe even before joining Haas and learnt a lesson.

The Mazepin family has a considerable interest in motor racing. It's far more than the formula of wealthy father paying for child to rise through karting and then see how far they can advance through single-seaters towards the holy grail of F1. In their case, the fortune that Mazepin Senior has earned thorough his Uralchem conglomerate puts him a in a different league. Up in the league of wealth that involves trying to buy an F1 team to call his own.

This might have been Force India, but he lost out to Lawrence Stroll in that attempt, with Lance's father renaming the team Racing Point and now Aston Martin.

Runner-up in the World Championship for KF karts in 2014, when 15, Nikita raced in both India's MRF Challenge and New Zealand's Toyota Racing Series single-seater championships over that winter before trying in Formula Renault in 2015.

Stepping up to F3 in 2016, his results were not spectacular with the family's Hitech team. He stayed in F3 for 2017 and began to gain ground, finishing 10th in the European series after claiming three podium finishes.

Nikita's 2018 season in GP3 was his best until last year's F2 campaign, as he grabbed four wins and eight further top-three results for the crack ART Grand Prix team to end the year as runner-up behind his team-mate Anthoine Hubert.

His first year in F2 was a bit of a wake-up call, as Nikita could rank just 18th after collecting only a pair of eighth place finishes, while his more experienced ART team-mate Nyck de Vries romped to the title.

With the aim both of staying sharp through the close-season and also landing the FIA superlicence that went with the title, Nikita then contested the Asian F3 championship. If he expected to take win after win as he stepped down a level, he was wrong and he failed to win even one of the 15 races which was a stain on his career record. Still, he knuckled down to a second year in F2 in 2020 and that more than erased that blemish, as described in the box-out below.

TRACK NOTES

Nationality:	**RUSSIAN**
Born:	**2 MARCH 1999, MOSCOW, RUSSIA**
Website:	**www.nikitamazepin.com**
Teams:	**HAAS F1 2021**

CAREER RECORD

First Grand Prix:	**2021 AUSTRALIAN GP**
Grand Prix starts:	**0**
Grand Prix wins:	**0**
Poles:	**0**
Fastest laps:	**0**
Points:	**0**
Honours:	**2018 GP3 RUNNER-UP, 2014 WORLD KF KART RUNNER-UP**

NIKITA'S BEST RACING SEASON YET

Whatever the size of his family fortune, Nikita can be quick in a racing car, and he seized his second season in the FIA F2 Championship and made clear progress to deliver more successfully than he did in the junior single-seater formulae. After failing to finish higher than eighth place in any F2 race in the 2019 season, Nikita really got things together with his family's Hitech Grand Prix outfit after enduring a dreadful opening two meetings, both at the Red Bull Ring, but then winning the opening races at the rounds held at Silverstone and Mugello. The Monza meeting was a disaster too and dented his title chances as he picked up just a single point, so he did well to bounce back and take his second win next time out at Mugello. Heading off to the final pair of meetings at Sakhir, he ranked only sixth, but it was really close on points with Yuki Tsunoda, Christian Lundgaard and fellow Russian Robert Schwartzman as they fought over third place. Despite taking a second, Nikita ended up fifth overall.

MICK SCHUMACHER

There's a resistance to second generation racers, as there's no reason that they should have any talent. Mick is different, as his track record shows that he's easily good enough in his own right, and 2021 will be his chance to show the world.

Mick held his nerve to land the F2 title and is in F1 on merit, not due to nepotism.

Very few racing drivers can resist putting their sons and daughters into a kart as soon as they're old enough. Even if the stopwatch suggests that the talent that they themselves possessed might have skipped a generation, many persevere. On rare occasions, though, there's every reason to push on and seven-time World Champion Michael loved watching Mick shine. In 2013, Mick ranked an impressive third at KF Junior Super Cup level in karting. Then, awfully, when they were skiing together, Michael suffered the tragic accident that left him with the severe brain injury he suffers to this day.

With family support, Mick pressed on and went better still in 2014, finishing as the runner-up in both the world and European KF Junior championships to show that he was more than ready to try car racing when he turned 16 in 2015.

His form in the ADAC F4 series based largely in Germany was strong but patchy as he won one of the three races at the opening round, then won no more through the rest of the campaign. In 2016, after a winter sojourn in India's MRF Challenge, Mick raced in the Italian series alongside his ADAC F4 campaign, wins came more easily as Mick spread 10 wins across the two series, placing second in both.

Another winter in the MRF Challenge kept him sharp in preparation for stepping up to the European F3 championship with Prema Racing and Mick soon showed that this was going to need to be a two-year programme. From 2017, when he scored no wins, Mick stepped up to be first to the finish eight times in 2018 and was a clear title winner. This was a hugely important result, as it silenced the critics who inevitably had thought of him first as a name – Schumacher – rather than a racer.

Signed as a member of the Ferrari Driver Academy in 2019, Mick enjoyed his first F1 test runs for Ferrari and Alfa Romeo. His main job, though, was competing in F2 and he won the reverse grid second race at the Hungaroring, but ended up outside the points too often to rank in the top 10. That was all put right last year.

TRACK NOTES

Nationality:	**GERMAN**
Born:	**22 MARCH 1999, VUFFLENS-LE-CHATEAU, SWITZERLAND**
Website:	**www.mickschumacher.ms**
Teams:	**HAAS F1 2021**

CAREER RECORD

First Grand Prix:	**2021 AUSTRALIAN GP**
Grand Prix starts:	0
Grand Prix wins:	0
Poles:	0
Fastest laps:	0
Points:	0
Honours:	**2020 FIA F2 CHAMPION, 2018 FIA F3 EUROPEAN CHAMPION, 2016 ADAC & ITALIN F4 RUNNER-UP, 2014 WORLD & EUROPEAN KF JUNIOR KART RUNNER-UP**

FAST AND CONSISTENT IN F2

The key to Mick's second year in the FIA F2 championship was his ability to gather points in almost every round. He built well on the experience he gained with Prema Racing in his rookie year at this penultimate stage on the single-seater racing ladder to shine through 2020. One helping factor in this was the fact that it was Mick's fifth year with the Italian team, as continuity can only be helpful, especially with a squad as well versed in winning as Prema. F2 continues to start the second race at each of its rounds with the top-eight finishers from the first race forming up on the grid in reverse order, so kudos goes to Mick for winning two of the opening races, at Monza and Sochi, the true indicator of a driver's form rather than the artificial lottery of the second race. Mick was under severe pressure from fellow Ferrari academy driver Callum Ilott and fast-finishing Yuki Tsunoda in the concluding rounds of the championship, but he kept his cool to end the year as a worthy champion.

WILLIAMS

Last May, with the world in the grip of Covid-19, news broke that this once great team was up for sale, and family involvement has now ended after four decades. A new year dawns in 2021, but it won't be an overnight fix for Williams.

George Russell qualified well through 2020 and will be hoping that new investment will enable him to get into the points this season.

The 71-year history of the World Championship shows that no team stays the same forever. Indeed, had this been the case, Frank Williams wouldn't have lasted in F1, as his team never looked like winning a thing in the middle 1970s. Then, however, it found its technical mojo thanks to technical chief Patrick Head and later a great sponsor and the wins began to flow from 1979 with its first F1 constructors' title the following year.

What followed as success bred success was a second spell at the tip of the F1 pyramid in the mid-1980s, a third spell in the early 1990s and a fourth towards the end of that decade. Yet, as with even the best teams before it, the pendulum of success swung away again and the lack of manufacturer support left the family-owned team prone to the savaging of even one poor season.

The decline set in and, 2015 aside when it ranked third ahead of Red Bull Racing, the downturn turned into a spiral of increasing debt and decreasing prize money. With Covid-19 preventing it from even going racing in the first half of last season, it reached its tipping point at which only the sale of the team would save it.

Lotus, Tyrrell and Brabham went from multiple World Champions to footnotes

KEY PERSONNEL & 2020 ROUND-UP

JAMES MATTHEWS
Former single-seater racer James returns to racing as one of the new board members after last year's take-over from the Williams family, having taken a 24-year break during which he built up the Eden Rock investment firm. The son of a former saloon racer, he was British and European Formula Renault champion in 1994, After two years in F3, he appropriated the name of the family's resort in Saint Barts for his own hedge fund, Eden Rock. He gained more fame by marrying Pippa, sister of the Duchess of Cambridge.

STILL TRYING HARD, BUT STILL FALLING SHORT
Watching Williams go about its tasks in 2020 was watching a team doing the best that it could with a car that wasn't up to scratch, this the result of a team whose budget has dwindled as a direct result of increasingly poor results. George Russell went for it in qualifying, but races were less competitive, while Nicholas Latifi did what he could in this ever more difficult cause. There will be changes to the management of the team following its purchase.

2020 DRIVERS & RESULTS

Driver	Nationality	Races	Wins	Pts	Pos
George Russell	British	16	0	0	18th
Nicholas Latifi	Canadian	17	0	0	21st
Jack Aitken	British	1	0	0	22nd

FOR THE RECORD

Country of origin:	**England**
Team base:	**Grove, England**
Telephone:	**(44) 01235 777700**
Website:	**www.williamsf1.com**
Active in Formula One:	**From 1972**
Grands Prix contested:	**000**
Wins:	**114**
Pole positions:	**128**
Fastest laps:	**133**

THE TEAM

Chairman:	**Matthew Savage**
Board members:	**Darren Fultz &**
	James Matthews
Chief executive officer:	**Jost Capito**
Acting team principal:	**Simon Roberts**
Chief technical officer:	**tba**
Chief designer:	**David Warner**
Deputy chief designer:	**Jonathan Carter**
Chief engineer:	**Doug McKiernan**
Head of aerodynamics:	**Dave Wheater**
Senior race engineer:	**Dave Robson**
Team manager:	**David Redding**
Test driver:	**tba**
Chassis:	**Williams FW44**
Engine:	**Mercedes V6**
Tyres:	**Pirelli**

in F1's history, but Williams will continue, albeit without family involvement.

Frank Williams was a racing driver who didn't have quite enough talent and definitely not enough money to make it to the top of the sport, so he turned to running cars for others in the late 1960s. Piers Courage twice finished second for him in 1969, and this helped to attract supercar manufacturer de Tomaso to join the show in 1970. It was a disaster and it turned into a tragedy when Courage was killed in the Dutch GP.

Williams did bounce back, but lacked the personal wealth to do things properly. He only got back on the pace when he was joined by designer Head in the late 1970s. Alan Jones started achieving decent results, then Head's ground-effects FW07 proved brilliant in 1979, with Clay Regazzoni taking the team's first win in the 1979 British GP, then Jones grabbing the 1980 drivers' title.

With decent backing at last, Williams grew from there. After Carlos Reutemann slipped up in the 1981 finale, albeit with

the team taking a second constructors' title in a row, Keke Rosberg landed Williams a second drivers' title in 1982.

A blow-out in the last race of 1986 cost Nigel Mansell the crown, but Nelson Piquet was crowned the following year.

Honda power was swapped for Renault engines in the early 1990s and Adrian Newey crafted a brilliant chassis to help Mansell storm to the 1992 title, with Alain Prost following suit in 1993. Damon Hill might have made it three in a row, but Michael Schumacher drove into him in the 1994 decider at Adelaide.

Hill then landed the 1996 crown and Jacques Villeneuve the one the following year, but then Williams' days of gunning for titles came to an end. There were still wins for Juan Pablo Montoya and Ralf Schumacher when BMW power was added, but Ferrari was pulling ever further clear of the pack as Michael Schumacher dominated.

As McLaren, Brawn GP and Red Bull Racing hit the front, Williams started to slide down the order, albeit with a shock

win for Pastor Maldonado in Spain in 2012. Sadly, as the rich grew richer, so the poor grew poorer and Williams' drop from the team to beat became ever more pronounced, with less and less money every year for development or securing the best personnel.

Still true racers at heart, Williams had become a shadow of its former self, unable to afford to end the malaise, and hopefully its new owners will invest enough to get it back on the right track, as F1 needs its great teams to remain and, from time to time, to shine.

"It's a new era for Williams and one that I'm excited to be playing a part in. I look forward to the challenge ahead as we look to take the team back to the front of the grid."

Simon Roberts

Back when Williams set the pace: Frank Williams is flanked by Nigel Mansell and Nelson Piquet.

» GEORGE RUSSELL

This will be George's third year of F1, and it's unlikely that he will stand out in what will remain F1's least competitive team. But, look closely, and his natural speed will be clear to see in qualifying. All he needs now is a top car.

George clearly needs a competitive car to gather the points his speed deserves.

One glance at George's career record shows that he is a driver who doesn't just win races but titles too. Karting yielded the European KF3 title, then his first year in single-seaters brought the British F4 crown and, because of this success, the prestigious McLaren *Autosport* BRDC Young Driver award.

This was only the beginning, though, as George impressed in European F3, ranking third behind Lance Stroll and Maximilian Guenther at his second attempt, suggesting that he was very good but not yet the pick of the pack.

When George graduated to GP3 in 2017, he returned to title-winning ways and did so at a canter. By this point, he was on Mercedes' books and gained some F1 experience, also getting a run with Mercedes-engined Force India.

Then came 2018, his year in F2, in which George dominated for ART Grand Prix by winning seven of the 24 races to leave fellow Brits Lando Norris and Alex Albon some way back in second and third. Very few drivers manage to win this last category before F1 at the first attempt and the fact that George made this unusual feat look so easy was a clear indication of his talent.

George was duly placed at Williams for his debut season in F1. This once dominant team had slid to be very much the tail-end team, but he raced for experience and came out ahead of his immediate yardstick, the experienced Robert Kubica. A best result of 11th place in the German GP left him just out of the points, but George had done enough to stay on for 2020.

After a second atypical year in which he found himself scrapping at the tail of the field, George at least gained some kudos away from the track when he overcame Charles Leclerc and Alex Albon in the Virtual Grand Prix series.

Keeping his spirits up through a third year with Williams might be hard, but he's an upbeat individual and knows that there could be an opening with Mercedes in 2022 as Valtteri Bottas was re-signed on a one-year contract.

TRACK NOTES

Nationality:	**BRITISH**
Born:	**15 FEBRUARY 1998, KING'S LYNN, ENGLAND**
Website:	**www.georgerussellracing.com**
Teams:	**WILLIAMS 2019-21, MERCEDES 2020**

CAREER RECORD

First Grand Prix:	**2019 AUSTRALIAN GP**
Grand Prix starts:	**38**
Grand Prix wins:	**0**
	(best result: 9th, 2020 Sakhir GP)
Poles:	**0**
Fastest laps:	**1**
Points:	**3**
Honours:	**2018 FORMULA 2 CHAMPION, 2017 GP3 CHAMPION, 2015 F3 MASTERS RUNNER-UP, 2014 BRITISH F4 CHAMPION & McLAREN AUTOSPORT YOUNG DRIVER AWARD, 2012 EUROPEAN KF3 KART CHAMPION**

SHOWING CLEAR SPEED ALONG THE WAY

The Williams FW43 was not the pick of the field, let's be clear about that. It was, in short, the slowest of the 10 models that went out to go for gold. Such was its performance deficit to the two Mercedes F1 W11s that George had to get his thrills some other way as he plotted how to wring the maximum from his car to get it up towards the points. He knew that this would require many of his rivals in faster cars to stumble, but he gave it his best shot. Qualifying was his happiest hunting ground and he worked miracles in that, peaking with 11th on the grid for the Styrian GP. Then followed the regular storyline of pushing perhaps harder than he ought as he tried to maintain position in the races, with qualifying pace counting for little as the race wore on. There were accidents as he pushed too hard, cruelly falling off during a safety car period at the Emilia Romagna GP when set to score. When Lewis Hamilton missed the Sakhir GP, George took his place at Mercedes and deserved to win, but was denied.

NICHOLAS LATIFI

This Canadian racer settled in well with Williams in his debut season. He didn't have the pace of team-mate George Russell over a single lap, but he showed great consistency through a grand prix distance and a good racing brain.

Nicholas raced well in 2020 and will surely build on that first year of F1 experience.

All of Nicholas's rivals look back at their years of racing karts, making racing part of their DNA by the time they graduated to single-seaters. For Nicholas, it was different, as he only dabbled in karts and elected to dive almost directly into car racing as soon as he was old enough to do so. This began with F3 in 2012 when he was 16, and perhaps it wasn't a wise choice to bypass the starter-level series, but he showed pace and claimed one win in the poorly-supported Italian series.

Next came an off-season campaign in New Zealand's Toyota Racing Series and then the far more competitive European F3 championship in 2013 and his lack of serious racing experience left him wanting. This was always going to be a two-year project, perhaps even three because of his lack of experience, but 10th place in 2014 as Esteban Ocon dominated wasn't what he had hoped for.

So, Nicholas and his family assessed the scene and opted for more powerful cars for 2015, with Nicholas racing in Formula Renault 3.5 and then in some late-season GP2 races too. Neither was a great success.

However, as money has never been an issue for this son of a Canadian industrialist, he was able to continue to refine his craft and so claimed his first GP2 podium in 2016.

Then F1's feeder formula changed its name from GP2 to F2 and Nicholas started to shine, taking his first win at Silverstone and ending the year fifth overall as Charles Leclerc dominated. In 2018, he won again, but this time ranked only ninth, thus hardly staking a claim on an F1 seat.

Nicholas's final year of F2, in 2019, was his most successful, as he started by winning three of the first five races and ended the year as runner-up to Nyck de Vries. Alongside this, his F1 involvement grew as he was put on Williams' books as reserve driver and participated in six free practice sessions at grands prix and also spent considerable time on simulator work for the team, all of which was invaluable experience.

TRACK NOTES

Nationality:	**CANADIAN**
Born:	**29 JUNE 1995,**
	TORONTO, CANADA
Website:	**www.nicholaslatifi.com**
Team:	**WILLIAMS 2020-21**

CAREER RECORD

First Grand Prix:	**2020 Australian GP**
Grand Prix starts:	**17**
Grand Prix wins:	**0 (best result: 11th,**
	2020 Austrian GP, Italian GP, Emilia
	Romagna GP)
Poles:	**0**
Fastest laps:	**0**
Points:	**0**
Honours:	**2019 F2 RUNNER-UP**

A SOLID DEBUT YEAR IN FORMULA 1

Examine the driver against driver tally in qualifying through the 2020 season and Nicholas failed to match up to his Williams team-mate George Russell, with an eventual score of 0 to 16 in favour of the Englishman. George already had a year of F1 under his belt so was expected to come out ahead, but Nicholas's confidence would have been boosted on the few occasions when he started nearer the front of the grid than George. What Nicholas needed to do principally was to get out onto the tracks, learn the ones he'd never visited before, and lay down good foundations for an F1 career that his family's investments will always be able to afford him. In this task, he did well, especially by grabbing 11th place in the opening race in Austria and then again at Monza and Imola. These were races of attrition, though, and indeed he was the final runner in that opening round. But he was still circulating and all he needed was one more retirement and he'd have claimed an invaluable point for Williams. His run at Imola was definitely his best 11th place finish as he left four others in his wake.

TALKING POINT: HOW HAMILTON RANKS AGAINST F1'S GREATS

With seven F1 titles and an almost always successful 14-year F1 career, it's no surprise at all that Lewis Hamilton is at the top of almost all lists of F1 stats. His tally is remarkable, but comparison isn't always fair, as drivers in F1's early years did fewer races, scored fewer points for a win and faced death if they crashed.

Who is the greatest F1 driver is the eternal debate among the sport's fans. Looking across 71 years of F1, the numbers show that it comes down to a head-to-head between Hamilton and Michael Schumacher, two drivers who raced against each other for just three years but both claimed seven F1 drivers' titles. Judge the record books by the stats on wins, pole positions, fastest laps and points scored, and it tends to be either of their names at the top of any of these tables. At the end of 2020, Hamilton is top for the most wins (95), poles (98) and points (3,778), with Schumacher still atop the tables for fastest laps (76) and most wins in a season (13).

Yet, there's more to F1 than just numbers. Take a driver considered the pick of the late 1960s who was capable of winning in anything: Jochen Rindt. Tragically, he was killed at Monza in 1970 and so never knew that he had done enough to be World Champion. For all his natural pace, his career didn't start with a top team and was short, which is why he ranks only 119th for grands prix started, 44th for wins, 34th for poles, 68th for fastest laps and 79th for points scored, yet he was one of the very best. Hamilton, on the other hand, went straight in with a top team, missing out on winning the F1 title at his first attempt by a single point. Schumacher became champion in his third full season.

The passage of time buries some of F1's greatest names way down the lists, below drivers who might not have won many grands prix, let alone a title. Take the table for most wins at the start of 2000, and Alain Prost is at the top on 51, with Schumacher second and Ayrton Senna third. Ten years later, and Schumacher was now on top, with 91 after a prodigious decade with Ferrari. Hamilton was way down the charts at this point, on 14. In 2020, Hamilton toppled Schumacher in wins and tied him with seven titles, with Prost and Senna, winners of four and three titles apiece, slipping to fourth and fifth. Only someone with little knowledge of F1 would think that this made them only fourth or fifth best behind the wheel.

Actually, the grands prix wins record has five-time World Champion Juan Manuel Fangio down in 11th, with 24 wins, but all came between 1951 and 1958, an era when he was all but untouchable. Add to this that the driver who acted as his pupil then, Stirling Moss, clocked up only 16 wins before his career-ending shunt in 1962 and there's a definite madness to the use of stats, as Moss was able to win in anything, but was often with the wrong team at the wrong time.

A typical F1 season in the 1950s had only eight grands prix before expanding to 16 from the early 1970s. Over the past decade, 20 or more has become usual, facilitating the speedier boosting of any tally.

Another fact was that only the top five finishers scored points until 1960, then the top six until 2003, when the allocation was spread to the first eight finishers, before later being given all the way down to 10th. On that basis, it's easy to see how F1's earlier stars had less of a chance to notch up impressive figures. As for the points on offer, a win was typically worth nine points and only got boosted to 10 in 1991, then 25 in 2010. A second-place finish was worth six points in the days of Jim Clark and Jackie Stewart, but that is the reward for seventh place today.

In many ways, it's best to analyse by percentage. For example, Fangio grabbed his 24 wins from just 51 grand prix starts for a strike rate of 47%, helped by the fact that he had only one down season as he racked up his five titles between 1951 and 1957, and this was in 1952 when he suffered a neck injury and didn't race.

So, are Hamilton and Schumacher definitively the best? I'll leave that to you to decide, but stats definitely don't tell you the true story. After all, Jim Clark, untouchable from the mid-1960s until his death in 1968, ranks well for wins (27, 10th) and poles (33, 5th), but is only 37th for points scored. See what I mean?

See the Formula One Records chapter starting on p120 for more stats.

Opposite top: Michael Schumacher makes his F1 debut in the 1992 Belgian GP.

Opposite middle: Lewis Hamilton's first win for Mercedes was in Hungary in 2013.

Opposite bottom left: Hamilton and Schumacher together in 2012.

Opposite bottom right: Hamilton with his winner's trophy at the 2020 Spanish GP.

TALKING POINT: **NEW OWNERS FOR WILLIAMS AFTER 43 YEARS**

How times change. Frank Williams was little more than a one-man band when he entered F1 in 1968 to run Piers Courage. Success took a time in coming but, from 1979, the wins flowed and titles too. Then came the fall from grace and family involvement is now over as the team is owned by venture capitalists.

Frank Williams was the name above the door of a team that claimed nine F1 constructors' titles and seven drivers' titles. Dorilton Capital is the new owner and it is hoped that its investment in the team will put Williams back on track.

This once great team that was the best of all for parts of the 1980s and the 1990s had become an also-ran. Since last having works engines in 2005, it had to pay for its engines and its continued failure to gather points meant that its prize money dwindled alarmingly, especially after ranking last in 2018 and 2019.

Something had to change and in May 2020 the team was put up for sale. By the end of August, a deal was done, and the Williams family's involvement came to an end. Sir Frank's daughter Claire knew this was an intensely personal matter, but the deputy team principal was pragmatic when the strategic review was carried out. "It proved that both F1 and Williams have credibility and value. When we started this process, we wanted to find a partner who shared the same passion and values, who recognized the team's potential and who could unlock its power. In Dorilton, we know we have found people who respect the team's legacy and will do everything to ensure it succeeds in the future.

"As a family, we have always put our team first. Making the team successful again and protecting our people has been at the heart of this process from the start."

Dorilton chariman Matthew Savage commented from its New York base: "We are delighted to have invested in Williams and we are extremely excited by the prospects for the business. We believe that we are the ideal partner for the company due to our flexible and patient investment style that will allow the team to focus on its objective of returning to the front of the grid."

Patrick Head, Frank's totemic technical chief from the formation of Williams Grand Prix Engineering in 1977, commented on why Williams fell to the bottom of the F1 pile and stayed there, saying that there had recently been a lack of technical leadership: "The team has had a stream of technical leaders, some of whom had skills but haven't been appropriate for leading a company like Williams."

Head should know as he made a huge impact when he joined Williams in the 1970s when teams were a fraction of the size that they are today and so good personnel then made even more of an impact. Put simply, Williams ran the team and Head handled the technical side and did so with both skill and decisiveness.

When Head talks, you should listen, as his expertise made Williams the pick of the pack for several spells as he assembled a trusted crew of engineers and aerodynamicists to help realize his visions. They worked supremely, as shown from the team's breakthrough win for Clay Regazzoni in 1979 then Alan Jones becoming its first champion in 1980. Nigel Mansell was then only denied by a puncture in 1986, before Nelson Piquet got the job done in 1987.

Honda took its engines to McLaren, but Williams was strong enough to strike back with Renault power in 1992 when Mansell dominated in the outstanding Adrian Newey-designed FW14B, then Alain Prost repeated the feat in 1993, with Damon Hill top in 1996 and Jacques Villeneuve in 1997.

However, no team keeps winning forever and Williams was confined to wins rather than titles after that, but even that stopped after its last win in 2012. The reason for this appears to have been not having the right group running the technical side. In 2018, its FW41 struggled due to flaws with its simulation work. Then, in 2019, Paddy Lowe was sacked for not having its new car ready for testing. Clearly, Lowe wasn't solely to blame and the new owners will have to be patient as they assemble the right people to solve its problems, perhaps hiring someone from outside F1, like McLaren did when it brought in Andreas Seidl from Porsche's sports-prototype programme.

The team will continue to be based at Grove in Oxfordshire with the current management team kept in place for the immediate future.

Opposite top left: Chief designer Adrian Newey chats to Nigel Mansell as team owner Frank Williams listens in.

Opposite top right: Claire Williams.

Opposite centre: Alan Jones won for Williams at Brands Hatch in 1980.

Opposite below: George Russell just missed out on points at Mugello last year.

TALKING POINT: CIRCUITS THAT COULD HOST A GRAND PRIX

The scramble to rearrange last year's World Championship calendar after the original one was decimated by the spread of the pandemic threw into light the fact that there are circuits beyond the regulars that are more than worthy of hosting F1. Here are some others that have the requisite grade to do the job.

Mugello and the Algarve International Circuit grabbed the opportunity to host a round of the World Championship for the first time last year and they provided interest with their gradient change. It was great, too, to have Imola, the Nurburgring and Istanbul Park back on the F1 roster as health restrictions prevented many of the 22 World Championship venues from hosting their rounds.

This got F1 fans talking about which other circuits were up to the standard required – FIA Grade One – to host a grand prix if required. Fanciful talk It might have been, but the appeal of some less than specifically-created tracks, old school even, has a strong pull.

The list of suitable circuits includes a further nine that have hosted the World Championship before: Buddh International, Estoril, Fuji, Hockenheim, Indianapolis Motor Speedway, Jerez, Korea International Circuit, Magny-Cours and Sepang.

Sepang always had its fans when it hosted the Malaysian GP between 1999 and 2017 and it's still seen as one of the best layouts penned by F1 circuit architect Hermann Tilke. The tropical weather could throw in a curveball too, as when it rains here it really rains.

However, check the FIA circuit rankings, and there are some surprising further options, some of which most F1 fans will never have heard of and all of which would certainly offer the World Championship the interest of a new backdrop. This list of potential new venues numbers the following nine tracks: Aragon, Buriram, Dubai, Fiorano, Kuwait Motor Town, Kymi Ring, Losail, Moscow Raceway and Valencia.

Of these, Buriram's Chang International Circuit in Thailand is one of the most frequently used, hosting national and international series both for two-wheeled and four-wheeled machinery, with Japan's well-supported Super GT series its most prestigious visitor. Cut out of a jungle plot on the edge of the city, it also has a drag strip and a top division football stadium.

Aragon in Spain has little apart from its track, but remains very popular for motorbike racing, with two-wheeled competition still more popular in Spain.

The Dubai Autodrome missed the boat after being opened in 2004 with the hope of hosting F1, but it has matured into a great facility that has the biggest day of its season with its well-supported 24-hour GT race each January.

Like Dubai, Qatar also yearned for the image boost from welcoming the World Championship and its Losail circuit also opened in 2004, but its main fare has been Moto GP. Kuwait didn't want to be left behind and commissioned Tilke to design a circuit. This opened in 2019, but Kuwait Motor Town looks more likely to be a home to regional racing.

Fiorano is a world-class facility for one reason alone: it's Ferrari's test circuit. Built in 1972 as a place where Enzo Ferrari could watch his cars from his house, it has been updated ever since, but now that F1 testing is severely limited it's used more for the company's road cars.

The quest for Russia to host a grand prix began in the 1990s, and various projects were considered before Tilke designed the Moscow Raceway. It opened in 2012 but F1 never came its way and it has been used since to host national and international meetings, while Sochi got to be Russia's F1 home.

The Valencia circuit in question is a permanent facility and not to be mistaken the city's street circuit visited by F1 between 2008 and 2012. This circuit came first but, apart from holding F1 tests when close-season testing was still a thing, that's been its only taste of F1 and the street circuit around the city's dock area was thought a more attractive option.

The wild card, in every sense, has to be the Kymi Ring. Cut out of the Finnish forests and located 110km north-east of Helsinki, it is the least likely place for a world-class track. It was built to attract MotoGP fans rather than F1 and is probably an attractve ride up from the capital.

So, the conversation will rage on about which other circuits would add to the F1 mix by their inclusion.

Opposite top: Ferrari's Fiorano test track is top spec, but remains just for Ferrari's own use. It also has no grandstands.

Opposite centre: Dubai Autodrome holds a 24-hour GT race every January.

Opposite bottom: Mark Webber against Sebastian Vettel at Istanbul Park in 2010.

TALKING POINT: **HOW DRIVERS KEPT BUSY THROUGH LOCKDOWN**

When the drivers arrived in Australia last March, they had no idea that the race wouldn't happen and that the pandemic would keep them off the tracks until June. In the interim, many turned to the virtual world and they loved how the competition they found there kept them match fit through this enforced time away.

Over the years, many drivers have decried time that they have to spend on a simulation rig to develop their cars, when they would far rather be out on the circuits. Yet, in recent years, testing has gone from something done almost every other week to something that is all but outlawed, which is why simulation work needs to be done. Most F1 aces consider it to be a necessary evil, preferably carried out by a test driver. That, though, has all changed due to the pandemic.

The platform on which the F1 drivers went racing was the Virtual Grand Prix series, a division of the F1 Esports series that had been running since 2017. With the younger F1 drivers being notably keen, viewing figures soon soared, as fans watched to see who would come out on top as they raced from their homes, sitting in rigs fronted with monitors, a steering wheel, pedals and with a race seat. Their input was shown through cameras looking back at them and their efforts were obvious, their competitiveness shining through.

Charles Leclerc was the early pace-setter, winning the rounds at Melbourne and Shanghai, but then Alex Albon enlisted the help of online racer Marcel Kiefer who had just won the F1 ESports Pro Series Brazilian GP. Kiefer helped the Red Bull Racing star to develop his sim racing craft. "I'm known in the sim racing community as Alex's technician/engineer," explains the German. "I help him via team radio and give strategic calls, like the right number of revs for the start and when to overtake. I'm fortunate to work with a talent like Alex, as he nails every bit of advice at the first attempt." His advice clearly, worked, as Albon went on to win at Interlagos.

Fellow British ace George Russell then came on strong, with wins at Barcelona, Monaco, Baku and Montreal to put his stamp on the championship in a way that he hasn't had a hope of doing with Williams in the real world. This landed him the title and gave him bragging rights over Lando Norris – who raced everything online from Indycars to Australian V8s – Stoffel Vandoorne, Sergio Perez, Pierre Gasly and Antonio Giovinazzi. By the end of the series, there had been more than 30 million hits.

Russell summed up what the title meant: "It may not be the real thing, but it's been such a buzz battling for wins with the lads again these past few months. I'd missed that feeling."

Another series that caught the eye was Rokit The Race All-Star Series, in which Fernando Alonso, Jenson Button, Emerson Fittipaldi and Juan Pablo Montoya did battle in virtual Brabham BT44s, suggesting the age of the game's developer is close to 60 as this wonderful car was raced in the mid-1970s.

Online racers like Kiefer have been affiliated to F1 teams for the past few years and some not only enter a squad of drivers in sim racing but even employ them to work on their simulation rigs, with Williams' Sami-Matti Trogen competing in rallying and the Nurburgring long-distance races to keep his hand in. Former Red Bull sim racer Cem Bolukbasi contests the GT4 European series, mixing virtual with real.

The cross-over is stronger than you would imagine, not just in terms of participation but also in the transfer of skills, and the knowledge doesn't flow only from F1 to sim racing, as race engineers were able to get involved and felt that it had kept them sharp, allowing them to keep honing their thoughts on set-up and race strategy. BMW thought so highly of online racing that it encouraged its drivers and engineers to get involved.

Online racing has a life of its own, and the uninitiated were shocked by its scale. For example, a virtual version of the Nurburgring 24 Hours had to run 55 parallel games so that it could accommodate the 1,400 four-driver teams that entered.

Online racing was given a huge boost as fans craved something to watch while racing was sidelined, but its appeal grew so much that not only will drivers make it part of their close-season, but so will the fans. In truth, if the virtual racing is good, it's easy to get so caught up that it can, for a moment, feel like the real thing.

Opposite top: The F1 stars learnt a lot from the regular F1 Esports racers.

Opposite centre left: Williams racer George Russell came on strong to take the title.

Opposite centre right: A screenshot from F1 2020.

Opposite below: The F1 Esports series proved to be a major hit in 2020.

F1 2020
THE OFFICIAL VIDEOGAME

WE. RACE. ON.

Bahrain Virtual Grand Prix
Sunday 22 March
2000 GMT

F1 Esports ▶ YouTube twitch

» KNOW THE TRACKS 2021

There are a record 23 grands prix planned for this year's Formula One World Championship, more than any season before it, but whether all of them get to be held is anyone's guess. What 2020 showed though is that the organizers might have to rearrange the order and indeed the venues according both to whether and where the pandemic continues to prevail.

If last year was one of necessity in the World Championship, this year's plans are about trying to return to normality, albeit with an expanded season required to make up some of the losses incurred in 2020 when just 17 of the 22 grands prix were held because of the restrictions caused by the global pandemic.

The likely order of races for the season ahead is Australia, Bahrain, China, an as-yet unconfirmed venue on 25 April, Spain, Monaco, Azerbaijan, Canada, France, Austria, Great Britain, Hungary, Belgium, Netherlands, Italy, Russia, Singapore, Japan, United States, Mexico, Brazil, Saudi Arabia (a new event) and finally Abu Dhabi.

This calendar isn't that different to what was planned for 2020, albeit with the Dutch GP's long-awaited F1 return not only missing last year but being moved towards autumn so that it can be combined in a double-bill with the Belgian GP the previous weekend. Indeed, the pairing of races is increasingly essential, simply to squeeze the 23 grands prix into the calendar year. Gone are the days when the World Championship had just 16 grands prix, largely held on alternate weekends. Now, F1 team personnel have to be on the road far more, travelling further and further from home increasingly often.

A grand prix had been planned at a new circuit in Hanoi in 2020, but Covid-19 got in the way of that. Disappointingly, the postponement turned into a missed opportunity as the event promoter was arrested for alleged misappropriation of state documents. The event's removal from its slot on the provisional 2021 F1 calendar leaves a gap that may be filled by one of a trio of venues that were given a call-up to host grands prix last year, namely Imola, Istanbul and the Algarve International Circuit.

It just wouldn't be F1 if there wasn't talk of the venue for the United States GP, especially as Austin's Circuit of the Americas has been having a hard time financially, so not being able to host a grand prix last year hit it hard. Texan F1 fans in particular will be glad that it's back on the calendar, especially as talk of a second grand prix held in the USA surfaced again last year, specifically a return to the infield circuit at the Indianapolis Motor Speedway. This is because it became increasingly unlikely that races in either Miami or Las Vegas would ever reach fruition.

It had been expected that the Brazilian GP would move away from Interlagos to a new circuit near Rio de Janeiro, but this may never happen as Interlagos now has a new five-year contract.

The year's greatest novelty will be the penultimate grand prix, held on a street circuit in Saudi Arabia's capital, Jeddah. The enticing debut will be made extra spectacular by being held after nightfall.

For 2022, the sport's owners are talking of 23 grands prix, increasing to 24 in 2023 and 25 the year after that. However, the teams are not at all keen on this season extension because of the extra costs and, more importantly, the way that multiple consecutive weekends of racing exhaust their personnel.

As it stands, the 2021 F1 World Championship stretches from the third weekend in March to the first weekend in December. Seasons concluding in October have been confined to history and those months of close-season that gave the teams time to examine new technical regulations and then develop their new cars have been squeezed over recent decades. Close-season testing has been limited considerably in F1's eternal quest to cut down costs, making the jobs of designers and engineers all the more difficult. Should their initial design estimations be out, then there is precious little chance to rectify a major flaw before the opening grand prix of the season.

» MELBOURNE

With last year's World Championship being hit by Covid-19, the Australian fans at least got a glimpse of the cars before they were packed away. This year, they will get a race.

When Melbourne wrested Australia's round of the World Championship from Adelaide and said it was going to build a temporary circuit in a suburban park, it triggered protests. However, the race organizers met enough of their concerns to get the go-ahead for 1996 and the Albert Park venue has been part of the show ever since.

The main feature needing to be circumnavigated was the lake in the middle of the park. This dictated the layout and a clockwise course was laid around it. The first third of the lap is busy, with a tight Turn 1 feeding immediately into a more open Turn 2. What follows is typical of half of the circuit in that the short blast to Turn 3 is hemmed in by concrete barriers and shaded by trees, making the track feel constricted.

Turn 3 is one of the few likely overtaking spots, a 110-degree right with a limited view of its exit. Turn 4, which runs behind a sports stadium, is more open, but from Turn 5 to Turn 6 it's again enclosed by trees. Then, finally, out of an esse, the circuit begins to open out. First the trees are replaced with open grass areas, making everything brighter. Then, after the third gear right that is Turn 9, the drivers are challenged by a wonderful left-arcing sweep, with a golf course to their left and the lake to their right, hitting 190mph before slowing for the flicks through Turns 11 and 12, the pick of the corners.

After a short straight, the circuit reverts to the feel of the early part of its lap as it enters a tree-shaded run through a series of 90-degree turns before reaching the grandstands overlooking the pit straight.

INSIDE TRACK

AUSTRALIAN GRAND PRIX

Date:	**21 March**
Circuit name:	**Albert Park**
Circuit length:	**3.295 miles/5.300km**
Number of laps:	**58**
Email:	**enquiries@grandprix.com.au**
Website:	**www.grandprix.com.au**

PREVIOUS WINNERS

2010	**Jenson Button** McLAREN
2011	**Sebastian Vettel** RED BULL
2012	**Jenson Button** McLAREN
2013	**Kimi Raikkonen** LOTUS
2014	**Nico Rosberg** MERCEDES
2015	**Lewis Hamilton** MERCEDES
2016	**Nico Rosberg** MERCEDES
2017	**Sebastian Vettel** FERRARI
2018	**Sebastian Vettel** FERRARI
2019	**Valtteri Bottas** MERCEDES

Its first grand prix: F1's first visit to Albert Park in 1986 came close to being an upset as Jacques Villeneuve was heading to victory on his F1 debut, but his Williams was losing oil and so victory went to team-mate Damon Hill. **Its greatest grand prix:** Jenson Button's 2009 win takes the prize, as he won for a team that had been closed at the end of 2008. An 11th hour reprieve led by Ross Brawn saved Honda Racing and inspired thinking gave the Brawn BGP 001 a winning performance advantage. **Its closest finish:** When McLaren scored a one-two in 1998, with Mika Hakkinen beating David Coulthard by 0.702s, the result confused the fans. The drivers had a pre-race agreement that whoever led into the first corner ought to win, but Hakkinen misheard a radio message and pitted from the lead. Honour-bound to let him back past, Coulthard did so. **Local hero:** There have been some real Aussie greats, from Jack Brabham to Alan Jones and Mark Webber. The big question is who will follow in Daniel Ricciardo's wheeltracks. F3 star Oscar Piastri is the most likely contender. **What else races here:** Albert Park is used just once a year, with Australian V8s, the Porsche Carrera Cup and Formula Ford on a packed bill.

MELBOURNE GRAND PRIX CIRCUIT

Marina — Lauda — Clark — Hill — Waite — Ascari — Senna — Prost — Whiteford — Pit lane

4 155	7 275	7 295	3 130	6 255
8 300	7 265	7 300	8 315	7 260
4 185	4 175	4 150	2 90	3 110
8 310	8 320	5 215	4 190	

6 Gear   **150** Km/h   ⏱**1** Timing sector   ▭ DRS   ▣ DRS detection

2019 POLE TIME: HAMILTON (MERCEDES), 1M20.486S, 147.385MPH/215.954KPH
2019 WINNER'S AVERAGE SPEED: 134.187MPH/223.075KPH
2019 FASTEST LAP: BOTTAS (MERCEDES), 1M25.580S, 138.612MPH/223.075KPH
LAP RECORD: M SCHUMACHER (FERRARI), 1M24.125S 141.016MPH/226.944KPH, 2004

SAKHIR

This Bahraini circuit lost its F1 slot last year as the pandemic struck then enjoyed not one but two visits when the championship was rejigged For 2021, it's back to its regular early-season slot

BAHRAIN GRAND PRIX

Date:	**28 March**
Circuit name:	**Bahrain International Circuit**
Circuit length:	**3.363 miles/5.412km**
Number of laps:	**57**
Email:	**info@bic.com.bh**
Website:	**www.bahraingp.com.bh**

PREVIOUS WINNERS

2012	**Sebastian Vettel** RED BULL
2013	**Sebastian Vettel** RED BULL
2014	**Lewis Hamilton** MERCEDES
2015	**Lewis Hamilton** MERCEDES
2016	**Nico Rosberg** MERCEDES
2017	**Sebastian Vettel** FERRARI
2018	**Sebastian Vettel** FERRARI
2019	**Lewis Hamilton** MERCEDES
2020	**Lewis Hamilton** MERCEDES
2020	**Sergio Perez** RACING POINT

Riches from the extraction of oil have found their way into F1 across the decades, but the days of financing individuals like Jim Hall in the 1960s and team entrant Walter Wolf in the 1970s were dwarfed in the 21st century by nations made wealthy by black gold lavishing huge sums to host a round of the World Championship. Bahrain led the way in 2004, Abu Dhabi followed in 2009, then Azerbaijan in 2016.

A plot of land was selected to the south of capital Manama and no expense was spared in building a state of the art facility with giant grandstands, excellent team offices and hospitality areas. To make the circuit more interesting, the section around the pits is known as the oasis, as constant irrigation enables grass verges to survive. The rest is arid.

Of the circuits designed by Hermann Tilke since the late 1990s, this has an unusually good flow. The first two corners are tight and close together, providing exciting moments at the start. However, the best stretch is on the downhill return from the Turn 4 hairpin, with a three-turn sweeper from Turn 5 to Turn 7.

The tight right at Turn 8 is a popular passing point, with another chance coming at Turn 10 where the track doubles back to run behind the paddock.

Drivers enjoy the curving ascent from Turn 11 to Turn 13 and the sweep through the final two corners onto the pit straight enables the drivers of the fastest cars to catch a tow to top 200mph before braking for Turn 1 again. If done well, this is one of the best places for drivers to attempt to pull off a passing move.

Its first grand prix: It was all Ferrari on Sakhir's debut in 2004. Michael Schumacher led home team mate Rubens Barrichello in what was to be a dominant season for the German. Slowest qualifier Zsolt Baumgartner's Jordan was 6s off the pace.

Its greatest grand prix: With its grand prix held early in the year, inter-team battles are rare, as one team usually arrives with an advantage. This is why 2019's race is special as it featured a battle between the Ferraris and Mercedes, with Ferrari's Charles Leclerc pulling off some great overtaking to take the lead, only for Lewis Hamilton to win when the Ferrari stuttered.

Its closest finish: Ferrari's Sebastian Vettel kept Mercedes' Valtteri Bottas and Lewis Hamilton at bay in 2018 after running a long second stint at the end of which he was just 0.699s ahead.

Local hero: Single seater series don't excite Bahrainis, and it's the Middle Eastern Porsche Carrera Cup they love. Isa Al-Khalifa the pick of their pack.

What else races here: As the Middle Eastern racing scene has matured, the circuit is now busy through the winter hosting regional Porsche, Lamborghini, F3 and F4 series.

71

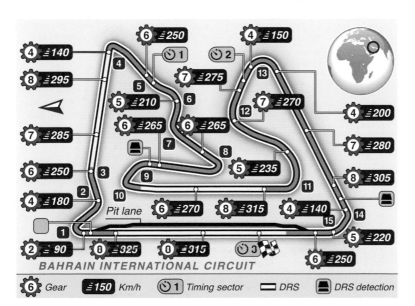

BAHRAIN INTERNATIONAL CIRCUIT

Pit lane

6 Gear | **≡150** Km/h | **1** Timing sector | DRS | DRS detection

2020 POLE TIME: **HAMILTON (MERCEDES), 1M27.264S, 138.732MPH/223.267KPH**
2020 WINNER'S AVERAGE SPEED: **63.917MPH/102.865KPH**
2020 FASTEST LAP: **VERSTAPPEN, BAHRAIN GP (RED BULL), 1M32.014S, 131.570MPH/211.742KPH**
LAP RECORD: **M SCHUMACHER (FERRARI), 1M30.252S 134.262MPH/216.074KPH, 2004**

SHANGHAI

Seventeen years after China hosted its first grand prix, the country Is still awaiting its first F1 racer, but the Shanghai International Circuit offers a track that is a great stage for their talents.

There seemed to be few constraints when the Shanghai International Circuit was built at the start of the 21st century, with everything about the track and its infrastructure feeling massive. That's what happens when a nation sees the circuit with which it has landed a place in the F1 World Championship as its calling card. This is especially so if the starting point in the circuit's design brief was that money was not an object, as the government would pay.

Built on marshy land to the north of China's business hub, the ever-expanding city has spread towards it in the past decade, but the circuit still feels as though it's on Shanghai's countryside fringe. With a giant grandstand and two huge bridges crossing the pit straight to the top of the pit building, the start straight is dwarfed, but then the drivers burst out of the shadow into a wonderful first corner sequence. This is three corners in a rapid sequence, with a sharp climb from Turn 1 to Turn 2 and then a steeper plunge into Turn 3, all of which allow plenty of passing on the opening lap of the race.

The next passing place comes at the Turn 6 hairpin. From here, drivers have to work hard through a run of esses before the next sharp corner at Turn 9.

Other passing spots are offered after the short straight to Turn 11. Best of all is the righthand hairpin, Turn 14, at the end of the unusually long back straight. This offers one of the best slipstreaming runs of the year and, after hitting 210mph on the approach, there's often a frantic struggle as drivers fight to pass or defend.

INSIDE TRACK

CHINESE GRAND PRIX

Date:	11 April
Circuit name:	Shanghai International Circuit
Circuit length:	3.390 miles/5.450km
Number of laps:	56
Email:	f1@china-sss.com
Website:	www.f1china.com.cn

PREVIOUS WINNERS

2010	**Sebastian Vettel** FERRARI
2011	**Lewis Hamilton** McLAREN
2012	**Nico Rosberg** MERCEDES
2013	**Fernando Alonso** FERRARI
2014	**Lewis Hamilton** MERCEDES
2015	**Lewis Hamilton** MERCEDES
2016	**Nico Rosberg** MERCEDES
2017	**Lewis Hamilton** MERCEDES
2018	**Daniel Ricciardo** RED BULL
2019	**Lewis Hamilton** MERCEDES

Its first grand prix: Ferrari was in control of 2004, with Michael Schumacher leading team-mate Rubens Barrichello when China made its bow near the end of the year. It was Barrichello who left as the inaugural winner, though, chased home by BAR's Jenson Button and McLaren's Kimi Raikkonen. Schumacher finished 12th after failing to set a time in qualifying, then clipping Christian Klien's Jaguar, picking up a puncture and then spinning.

Its greatest grand prix: It's rare to have three teams in with a shot, but this was the situation in 2018 when Mercedes, Ferrari and Red Bull were all in the mix, but Red Bull called the shots best and Daniel Ricciardo did the rest.

Its closest finish: In 2015, Lewis Hamilton beat Nico Rosberg by 0.714s in a Mercedes one-two, but Rosberg claimed that Hamilton had "backed him up" to Ferrari's Sebastian Vettel.

Local hero: F2 star Guanyu Zhou is at the front of the queue to be China's second F1 driver after Ma Qing Hua did a few practice sessions in 2012/2013.

What else races here: The Chinese racing scene is blossoming, with single-seater categories popular, but GT racing even more so.

SHANGHAI INTERNATIONAL CIRCUIT

Pit lane

6 Gear	150 Km/h	1 Timing sector	DRS	DRS detection

2019 POLE TIME: **BOTTAS (MERCEDES)**, 1M31.547S, 133.193MPH/214.355KPH
2019 WINNER'S AVERAGE SPEED: **123.483MPH/198.727KPH**
2019 FASTEST LAP: **GASLY (RED BULL)**, 1M34.742S, 128.702MPH/207.126KPH
LAP RECORD: **M SCHUMACHER (FERRARI)**, 1M32.238S 132.202MPH/212.759KPH, 2004

The sheer enormity of the grandstand and pit buildings is shown back in 2018 as Ferrari's Sebastian Vettel leads the field away.

» BARCELONA

The Circuit de Barcelona-Catalunya was given a reprieve in 2019 to keep its place on the calendar, and this year the home fans will not only have Carlos Sainz Jr in a Ferrari but also Fernando Alonso back in F1.

The Spanish GP has moved around since its first World Championship round in 1951. That was on a street circuit in the Pedralbes suburb of Barcelona, then purpose-built Jarama outside Madrid was used from the mid-1960s to 1981, interspersed with races around Barcelona's Montjuich Park, and then a spell at Jerez. Since the Circuit de Catalunya took over the race from 1991 it at last has a long-term home. Unfortunately, it was struggling to afford to host a grand prix and it took a €21m investment from the regional government to keep it in the World Championship after 2019.

The circuit located in rolling hills north of Barcelona was once F1's predominant testing venue, due to its wide range of corners and generally fine weather. Then in-season testing was all but banned and so visits are fewer.

The lap starts with a downhill run to the first corner which is the first part of a right/left esse that encourages many a driver to try an overtaking move on the opening lap. Some work, some don't.

A long, long uphill righthander follows and then the track doubles back before turning right again. Then, from Turn 5, it drops down towards the edge of the paddock before starting a climb to the lap's highest point at Turn 9, Campsa. This is the lap's most challenging corner as it's over a brow, making lines of sight difficult.

The infield straight is downhill to Turn 10 before the track snakes up the slope again before dipping through Turn 13 and falling away from there to a fiddly chicane that is the entry to the long blast on which drivers top 200mph before they brake for Turn 1, the prime place for passing.

INSIDE TRACK

SPANISH GRAND PRIX

Date:	**9 May**
Circuit name:	**Circuit de Barcelona-Catalunya**
Circuit length:	**2.892 miles/4.654km**
Number of laps:	**66**
Email:	**info@circuitcat.com**
Website:	**www.circuitcat.com**

PREVIOUS WINNERS

2011	**Sebastian Vettel**	RED BULL
2012	**Pastor Maldonado**	WILLIAMS
2013	**Fernando Alonso**	FERRARI
2014	**Lewis Hamilton**	MERCEDES
2015	**Nico Rosberg**	MERCEDES
2016	**Max Verstappen**	RED BULL
2017	**Lewis Hamilton**	MERCEDES
2018	**Lewis Hamilton**	MERCEDES
2019	**Lewis Hamilton**	MERCEDES
2020	**Lewis Hamilton**	MERCEDES

Its first grand prix: The first grand prix here, in 1991, was an easy win for Nigel Mansell for Williams, with the strength of that year's field shown by the 33 cars that turned up to try to qualify.

Its greatest grand prix: Seldom when a driver wins by a huge margin is a race considered great, but Michael Schumacher's victory for Ferrari in 1996 was touched by greatness as he won in the wet by 45s while his rivals spun off.

Its closest finish: The gap between Max Verstappen and Ferrari's Kimi Raikkonen was 0.616s in 2016 when the Dutch teenager shocked everyone by taking his first F1 win on his maiden outing for Red Bull Racing after promotion from Scuderia Toro Rosso.

Local hero: The gap between the F1 careers of "Fon" de Portago and Fernando Alonso was 44 years and in that period Spain produced not one grand prix-winning driver. Looking to follow Carlos Sainz Jr is Alex Palou who shone in Indycars in 2020.

What else races here: The rise of GT racing combined with the decline of touring cars has led to a change in the most frequent visitors, usually supported by single-seater categories F3 and F4.

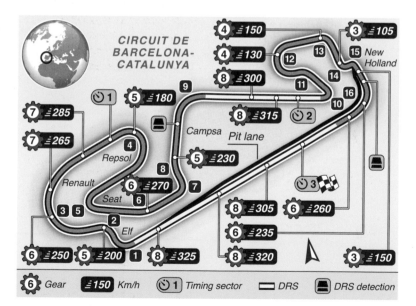

CIRCUIT DE BARCELONA-CATALUNYA

Campsa

Pit lane

Repsol

Renault

Seat

Elf

New Holland

6 Gear	150 Km/h	1 Timing sector	DRS	DRS detection

2020 POLE TIME: HAMILTON (MERCEDES), 1M15.584S, 137.766MPH/221.713KPH
2020 WINNER'S AVERAGE SPEED: 124.784MPH/200.820KPH
2020 FASTEST LAP: BOTTAS (MERCEDES), 1M18.183S, 133.186MPH/214.343KPH
LAP RECORD: BOTTAS (MERCEDES), 1M18.183S 133.186MPH/214.343KPH, 2020

MONACO

After a year without visiting Monaco, the teams, the fans and particularly the sponsors will be delighted to be returning to this wonderful but incredibly popular and prestigious anachronism of a circuit.

Compare Monaco to any modern F1 circuit and it is incredibly different, even when put against Baku and Singapore, the two other street circuits visited by the World Championship, as its lap is tighter, shorter and older.

Dating back to 1929, this circuit in the heart of Monte Carlo, with the harbour on one side and the castle above, is unmistakable, its backdrop so distinctive. Visit when the barriers have been dismantled, and it's hard to envisage a circuit being squeezed into the busy streets, but somehow it does, albeit with the teams' transporters having to be parked in a separate paddock.

The lap starts with a curving start/finish "straight" and the first turn, Ste Devote, has a kinked and narrow entry before turning the cars up a steep climb towards its highest point at Massenet before the cars fire out across Casino Square. The surrounding buildings grow ever taller as the last of the villas are replaced with apartment blocks, emphasizing the constricted feel for drivers as they look in desperation for a place to overtake. Down the slope to Mirabeau and then the hairpin in front of the Grand Hotel offer little scope.

The track drops through two righthanders onto the seafront. Then it's flat-out through the tunnel under the hotel and back into the light for the slope down to the Nouvelle Chicane where there is a chance to try to pass as they brake from 180mph.

No longer hemmed in by buildings, the track runs fast through Tabac then really challenges the drivers with the quick fire sequence around the swimming pool. The last few corners feel tighter still.

INSIDE TRACK

MONACO GRAND PRIX

Date:	**23 May**
Circuit name:	**Circuit de Monaco**
Circuit length:	**2.075 miles/3.339km**
Number of laps:	**78**
Email:	**info@acm.mc**
Website:	**www.acm.mc**

PREVIOUS WINNERS

2010	**Mark Webber** RED BULL
2011	**Sebastian Vettel** RED BULL
2012	**Mark Webber** RED BULL
2013	**Nico Rosberg** MERCEDES
2014	**Nico Rosberg** MERCEDES
2015	**Nico Rosberg** MERCEDES
2016	**Lewis Hamilton** MERCEDES
2017	**Sebastian Vettel** FERRARI
2018	**Daniel Ricciardo** RED BULL
2019	**Lewis Hamilton** MERCEDES

Its first grand prix: An accident triggered by Giuseppe Farina spinning on lap 1 removed nine of the 19 starters in 1950, with Juan Manuel Fangio going on to win for Alfa Romeo.

Its greatest grand prix: Three teams filled the top three places in 2012 when Red Bull Racing's Mark Webber led home Mercedes' Nico Rosberg and Ferrari's Fernando Alonso, covered by less than 1s. Webber started from pole and weathered pressure from Rosberg plus a late-race shower.

Its closest finish: In 1992, Monaco enjoyed one of its epic battles. It was all Nigel Mansell as he led from pole in his pace-setting Williams, heading for six wins from starts, but he pitted with seven laps to go, thinking he had a puncture. He then reduced his 5s deficit to Ayrton Senna to nothing and tried left and right, but the McLaren held on to win by 0.215s.

Local hero: Charles Leclerc has another rising Monegasque star following in his wheeltracks, his own brother, Arthur.

What else races here: Monaco's street circuit has been used only for the grand prix until the past decade, when the barriers are left in place every second year for a festival of historic racing.

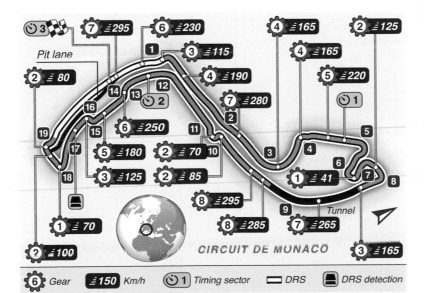

CIRCUIT DE MONACO

🕓 **3**	Gear	🏁	
	Pit lane		

Gear | Km/h | Timing sector | DRS | DRS detection

2019 POLE TIME: HAMILTON (MERCEDES), 1M10.166S, 106.385MPH/171.211KPH
2019 WINNER'S AVERAGE SPEED: 93.391MPH/150.298KPH
2019 FASTEST LAP: GASLY (RED BULL), 1M14.279S, 100.494MPH/161.730KPH
LAP RECORD: VERSTAPPEN (RED BULL), 1M14.260S 100.520MPH/161.772KPH, 2018

Singapore's Marina Bay Circuit provides one of F1's most dramatic backdrops, especially after nightfall.

» REVIEW OF THE 2020 SEASON

That the Formula One World Championship happened at all was a triumph for fleet-footed thinking and clever rearrangement. Despite the date changes and loss of five grands prix, the story remained the same, with Mercedes cruising to victory. Lewis Hamilton remained the class of the field and duly became the most successful F1 driver of all time as he raced to his seventh title.

The teams were assembled in Melbourne to kick off the 2020 World Championship when a few people in the paddock were found to be Covid-positive. There was no choice but to send everyone home. With the pandemic worsening rapidly, it meant that there was an entire reappraisal and a new set of grands prix, 17 rather than the original 22, starting in July.

So that the championship could be run

at all, the teams had to operate in "bubbles" and social-distancing observed at all other times. There were occasional positive tests, but F1 came through this severe test, even though some of the personnel felt drained by four triple-header sequences of races.

So, there was racing, but the downsides included the fact that the fans and media were largely kept away. On the plus side, a few circuits previously dropped by F1 – the

Nurburgring, Imola and Istanbul Park – and others that had never had the honour – Mugello and the Algarve International Circuit – provided welcome variety.

Despite all these alterations, the outcome was the same as in 2017, 2018 and 2019 in that Mercedes and Lewis Hamilton dominated. Sure, team-mate Valtteri Bottas won the opening round at the Red Bull Ring, but Lewis then rattled off three wins on the

trot to put himself back into the driving seat. There were trials and tribulations, but the wins kept on flowing and it was clear that the year was his. Bottas wasted his occasional poles with poor starts, but won in Russia as he fought to hold off Max Verstappen.

Verstappen was invariably the best of the rest for Red Bull Racing and he broke Mercedes' winning streak when he was first home in the 70th Anniversary GP at Silverstone. He could have won the weekend before at the British GP, but pitted for fresh tyres just as leader Hamilton's car had a blow-out on the final lap. Through the rest of the season, he kept on charging. Alex Albon started the season strongly, then fell away, before a late-season return to form.

The battle for third place in the constructors' championship was tight, and Racing Point moved to the head of the chasing pack late on thanks to Sergio Perez's wins, before McLaren pipped them.

McLaren kicked off its season with a first podium for Lando Norris in the Austrian GP and he raced strongly through the first half of the year. It had been announced that Carlos Sainz Jr was to be replaced by Daniel Ricciardo for 2021, but the Spaniard raced ever more competitively and came within a fraction of a second of winning the Italian GP as he rose up the table.

Renault appeared to turn a corner in 2020 and Ricciardo came out on top of the internal battle with Esteban Ocon, racing to third at the Nurburgring for its first podium since the 2015 Belgian GP. He was third at Imola before Ocon was second at Sakhir.

Ferrari had a power shortfall compared to 2019. Charles Leclerc led its attack, but his second place in the opening race was never repeated. Sebastian Vettel was increasingly off the pace before finding late-season form.

AlphaTauri will always remember 2020 fondly as the year the Italian team took its second win. Twelve years after Sebastian Vettel triumphed at Monza, Pierre Gasly did the same. Daniil Kvyat showed great fight by racing to fourth at Imola.

Alfa Romeo offered little and neither Kimi Raikkonen nor Antonio Giovinazzi could finish higher than ninth. Likewise, Haas F1 suffered from a lack of Ferrari horsepower and both Kevin Magnussen and Romain Grosjean suffered a similar fate.

Williams was very much the bottom team again last year, and worse, its overheads became too much and it had to seek a buyer. Despite this, George Russell in particular made progress but just missed out on points, while Nicholas Latifi also improved.

Lewis Hamilton was back after a race out with Covid symptoms, but he had no answer to the pace of Max Verstappen's Red Bull on his return, as the Dutch ace rounded out his season in style and McLaren vaulted Racing Point to rank third overall.

There was some surprise that Lewis Hamilton was back for this final round and he soon admitted that he remained short on energy. Either way, pole was not within his reach and it didn't go to team-mate Valtteri Bottas either, as Max Verstappen took the top spot for Red Bull Racing.

Verstappen led away and there seemed to be nothing Bottas could do about it. Overtaking has always been rare at Yas Marina, and when the safety car was triggered after 11 laps, so that Sergio Perez's Racing Point could be removed, any hope of a race decided by differing race strategy was expunged. Almost all the teams opted to pit for fresh tyres at the same time in order to run to the finish without another pitstop.

No matter what Bottas did, Verstappen had the answers. Perhaps Hamilton was potentially faster than his team-mate, but he remained third and, late in the race, felt his energy fall away.

Alex Albon tried to impress enough to keep the second Red Bull seat in 2021 and he passed Lando Norris early on for fourth and then ran close enough to Mercedes to hem them in. Behind him, fifth and sixth places for Norris and Carlos Sainz Jr were enough to propel McLaren past Racing Point into third place in the constructors' championship, a place change worth around £7.5 million in prize money, with Lance Stroll able only to finish 10th. There was a concern that Sainz Jr might be penalised for delaying Stroll enough in the pits to cost the Canadian places. However, he was cleared.

One driver who did things differently was Daniel Ricciardo, who stayed out longer than his rivals in his first stint. This helped him to have a shorter second stint on the softer tyre and so he was able to climb from 11th up to seventh.

116

YAS MARINA ROUND 17

DATE: **13 DECEMBER 2020**

Laps: **55** · Distance: **189.738 miles/305.355km** · Weather: **Warm & dry**

Pos	Driver	Team	Result	Stops	Qualifying Time	Grid
1	**Max Verstappen**	Red Bull	1h36m28.645s	1	1m35.246s	1
2	**Valtteri Bottas**	Mercedes	1h36m44.621s	1	1m35.271s	2
3	**Lewis Hamilton**	Mercedes	1h36m47.060s	1	1m35.332s	3
4	**Alex Albon**	Red Bull	1h36m48.632s	1	1m35.571s	5
5	**Lando Norris**	McLaren	1h37m29.374s	1	1m35.497s	4
6	**Carlos Sainz Jr**	McLaren	1h37m34.307s	1	1m35.815s	6
7	**Daniel Ricciardo**	Renault	1h37m42.393s	1	1m36.406s	11
8	**Pierre Gasly**	AlphaTauri	1h37m58.363s	1	1m36.242s	9
9	**Esteban Ocon**	Renault	1h38m09.714s	1	1m36.359s	10
10	**Lance Stroll**	Racing Point	1h38m11.383s	1	1m36.046s	8
11	**Daniil Kvyat**	AlphaTauri	54 laps	1	1m35.963s	7
12	**Kimi Raikkonen**	Alfa Romeo	54 laps	1	1m37.555s	15
13	**Charles Leclerc ***	Ferrari	54 laps	1	1m36.065s	12
14	**Sebastian Vettel**	Ferrari	54 laps	1	1m36.631s	13
15	**George Russell**	Williams	54 laps	1	1m38.045s	16
16	**Antonio Giovinazzi**	Alfa Romeo	54 laps	1	1m38.248s	14
17	**Nicholas Latifi**	Williams	54 laps	2	1m38.443s	18
18	**Kevin Magnussen !**	Haas	54 laps	2	1m37.863s	20
19	**Pietro Fittipaldi**	Haas	53 laps	3	1m38.173s	17
R	**Sergio Perez !**	Racing Point	8 laps/transmission	0	no time	19

FASTEST LAP: RICCIARDO, 1M40.926S, 123.096MPH/198.104KPH ON LAP 55 · RACE LEADERS: VERSTAPPEN 1-55
* 3-PLACE GRID PENALTY FOR CAUSING A COLLISION AT PREVIOUS RACE, ! MADE TO START AT REAR OF GRID FOR USING EXTRA POWER UNIT ELEMENTS

Max Verstappen leads Valtteri Bottas and Lewis Hamilton on the way to victory in Abu Dhabi.

Lando Norris crosses the line at the Abu Dhabi GP as his McLaren team-mates celebrate taking third place in the Constructors' Championship.

Niki Lauda put Ferrari back on the track in 1975 when he took the drivers' title and guided the team to the first of three constructors' titles in a row.

MOST FASTEST LAPS

DRIVERS

76	Michael Schumacher	(GER)	21	Gerhard Berger	(AUT)		Jackie Stewart	(GBR)
53	Lewis Hamilton	(GBR)	20	Nico Rosberg	(GER)	14	Jacky Ickx	(BEL)
46	Kimi Raikkonen	(FIN)	19	Damon Hill	(GBR)	13	Alberto Ascari	(ITA)
41	Alain Prost	(FRA)		Stirling Moss	(GBR)		Alan Jones	(AUS)
38	Sebastian Vettel	(GER)		Ayrton Senna	(BRA)		Riccardo Patrese	(ITA)
30	Nigel Mansell	(GBR)		Mark Webber	(AUS)	12	Rene Arnoux	(FRA)
28	Jim Clark	(GBR)	18	David Coulthard	(GBR)		Jack Brabham	(AUS)
25	Mika Hakkinen	(FIN)	17	Rubens Barrichello	(BRA)		Juan Pablo Montoya	(COL)
24	Niki Lauda	(AUT)	16	Felipe Massa	(BRA)	11	John Surtees	(GBR)
23	Juan Manuel Fangio	(ARG)	15	Valtteri Bottas	(FIN)	10	Mario Andretti	(USA)
	Nelson Piquet	(BRA)		Clay Regazzoni	(SWI)		Graham Hill	(GBR)
22	Fernando Alonso	(SPA)		Daniel Ricciardo	(AUS)		Max Verstappen	(NED)

CONSTRUCTORS

253	Ferrari	56	Alpine (including Toleman, Benetton, Renault*, Lotus* & Renault *)	14	Alfa Romeo
157	McLaren			13	Cooper
133	Williams	40	Brabham	12	Matra
84	Mercedes GP (including BAR, Honda Racing & Brawn GP)	22	Tyrrell	11	Prost (including Ligier)
		18	Renault	9	Mercedes
71	Lotus	15	BRM	7	March
68	Red Bull Racing		Maserati	6	Vanwall